GCSE: EXAMINING THE NEW SYSTEM

Edited by
TIM HORTON

Harper & Row, Publishers
London

Cambridge
Philadelphia
New York
San Francisco

Mexico City
São Paulo
Singapore
Sydney

First published 1986

Harper & Row Ltd
28 Tavistock Street
London WC2E 7PN

British Library Cataloguing in Publication Data
GCSE: examining the new system.
1. General certificate of secondary
education examination (Great Britain)
I. Horton, Tim
373.12'62   LB 3056.G7

ISBN 0-06-318360-9

Typeset by Inforum Ltd, Portsmouth
Printed and bound by Butler & Tanner Ltd, Frome and London

CONTENTS

CONTRIBUTORS

Paul Armitage is Principal Professional Officer for History and Social Science at the SEC. With Laurence Taylor he was the co-author of *GCSE: A Teacher's Guide – History*, published by the SEC and the Open University.

Patricia Broadfoot is a lecturer in Education at the University of Bristol and co-director of the DES-funded pilot Records of Achievement in Schools Evaluation (PRAISE) Project.

Barbara Hodgson is a Lecturer at the Institute of Educational Technology at the Open University, and was a member of the team which produced *GCSE: A Teacher's Guide – Science*, published by the SEC and the Open University.

Tim Horton is a Lecturer in Curriculum Studies in the School of Education of the Open University. He was formerly Research and Curriculum Development Officer for the National Union of Teachers serving on several curriculum and research bodies. He was a member of the SEC/OU Inset team.

Ian McNay is a Lecturer in the School of Education, the Open University.

Maggie MacLure is a Lecturer in Education at the University of East Anglia, and the author of *GCSE: A Teacher's Guide – English*, published by the SEC and the Open University.

Roger Murphy is a Lecturer in Education at the University of Southampton, where he is also Director of the Assessment and Examinations Unit.

Keith Orrell is a Senior Lecturer in the School of Education, Leeds Polytechnic, ex-director of the Schools Council Geography 14–18 Project, chief examiner for the Project, and a member of the SEC Geography Subject Panel.

David Pennycuick is a Lecturer in Education at the University of Sussex and was previously at the Assessment and Examinations Unit, University of Southampton.

Bill Prescott is a Senior Lecturer in the School of Education, the Open University, and was a member of the SEC/OU Inset Team.

Walter Roy is Headmaster of the Hewett School, Norwich, and Chairman of the London and East Anglian Group for the GCSE.

Brian Salter is Senior Research Fellow, Department of Education Studies, University of Surrey.

John Scarth is a Research Fellow in the School of Education, the Open University.

Peter Scrimshaw is a lecturer in the School of Education, the Open University. He was a member of the SEC/OU Inset team, and is chair of the Open University course, Purpose and Planning in the Curriculum.

Christine Shiu is a lecturer in Mathematics Education in the Faculty of Mathematics of the Open University. Until recently she taught in a Leicestershire Upper School (age range 14–18), and is helping to coordinate the development of resources for extended coursework in GCSE mathematics, for Mode 3 schemes based in Leicestershire schools.

Ted Tapper is Reader in Politics at the University of Sussex.

Lawrence Taylor is Adviser for Humanities, Berkshire County Council and was co-author with Paul Armitage of *GCSE: A Teacher's Guide – History*, published by the SEC and the Open University.

Harry Torrance is a lecturer in the Department of Education at the University of Southampton, and is attached to the Assessment and Examinations Unit. He is involved in research on school-based assessment and profiles.

Introduction
VACILLATION AND VISION
Tim Horton (*Open University*)

Proposals for the General Certificate of Secondary Education (GCSE) have survived the most turbulent period in eduation since the Second World War. Its advent, a decade after James Callaghan's Ruskin College speech, is interpreted in many different ways. To some, it expresses the resilience of a partnership in education – reform through a consensus, born in more optimistic times. To others, it represents a vital step in increasing the centralization of education – accountability through curricular, as well as financial, control mechanisms.

Ironies are plentiful. The visionaries of the nineteen-sixties who saw the Certificate of Secondary Education (CSE) as the precursor to more radical reform, involving common certification for all school leavers, are now often the most sceptical. Sixteen is no longer the common leaving point for students as the new examination system marks out, for most pupils, only one stage of a career in education. Again, new syllabuses, ushered in by schemes for vocational preparation, seem to offer greater relevance to the needs of many students. Yet it is as a football in the politics of education from 1985 that the GCSE became imprinted on the mind. Its introduction was a major bargaining counter in the complex negotiations over teachers' pay and conditions, and the touchstone for arguments over capitation in schools and education committees.

The disputes over its introduction have produced waves that may take years to calm. Yet the GCSE carries implications for teachers and students that the heated debates have often masked. The contributors to this book have taken a look at the new system from several perspectives – above the battle, but not ignoring it. Taken together, their writings stake out the prospects for its future success.

The first section of the book considers the changes upon the various stakeholders with interests in the examination system – particularly the examination boards, teachers and their professional organizations, and the

Department of Education and Science. Roger Murphy points to the past secretiveness of the boards and their emphasis on administrative facilitation rather than bold innovation. He suggests that the 'shotgun weddings' initiated by the 1978 Waddell Report have not led to any major change in these stances, although the new examination groups have developed some differences in character. A novel factor, however, is the sharper commercial and competitive environment that has been introduced. Walter Roy detects the emergence of two models of control represented by the new examining groups – one favouring a unitary, the other a federal, approach. In both he sees a challenge for teachers seeking to exert their influence. He argues that the governance of examination groups could potentially restore to teachers the influence they lost with the abolition of the Schools Council in 1984.

Roy underlines the historical importance of the major teacher unions in the vanguard of advocates of a common 16+ for over twenty years. His criticism over the current low resourcing of schools gives added dimension to the scale of the individual efforts of teachers to make the old and new systems more effective.

Brian Salter and Ted Tapper's analysis suggests that the battle for control over the examination system has already been lost and that long-standing ambitions within the DES have triumphed. Departmental ascendancy was achieved, they argue, only through an alliance with the overtly political forces of the New Right, thus fracturing the old partnership.

Peter Scrimshaw diagnoses similar rearrangements in the control of education as having major impact for the curriculum *through* the examination system. For Scrimshaw the erection of national criteria is critical. It is not simply that several subjects have been tightly defined, but rather that their formal alteration will require the assent of the Secretary of State, whose position is strengthened by the arrangement whereby examining groups compete with each other. The struggle for influence is not final and might be challenged if the Department's former partners can regroup and use new information systems to their own advantage.

Scrimshaw's attention to the *political* significance of the techniques of assessment and to the establishment of general and subject criteria adds poignancy to the next set of contributions. In two contributions, I consider the general implications of the emphasis on coursework and positive assessment in the new system. In the light of the cursory and often ill-fated plans for in-service work before the examination, these aspects of the new system have proved most vexing to teachers, particularly to those lacking experience of joint schemes under the old arrangements.

In five contributions, experts in specific subject areas consider the implications for practice. In general, they are hopeful about the future for

English, Mathematics, Science, History and Geography. Each account analyses the antecedence of any changes, many of which strengthen current concerns for the assessment of *processes* in learning rather than the measurement of *products*. There are several expressions of concern about the sheer volume of administration that coursework assessment brings about, and anxieties are expressed about the directions taken in formulating grade criteria for subjects. At the time that these contributions were made, the nature of grade criteria was still largely uncertain, but it is anticipated that their implementation in the years ahead could have implications no less dramatic than those in the first two years of the new system.

The need to redirect professional practice, so much at the centre of ministerial thinking in the 1980s, provides the focus for the three contributions in the third section of the book. If change *is* desirable, which strategy (or combination of strategies) is most likely to achieve it? Three alternative mechanisms can be considered. The first, a 'cascade' model of INSET, attends to the need for urgency and, at the same time, the number of teachers to be involved. The second refers to the commonly stated view that teachers adhere to the detailed guidelines of syllabuses and are not often inclined towards extemporization. The third is the 'root and branch' approach represented by school-based curriculum development which, through focusing on the actual practice of schools, addresses the inter-relatedness of characteristics of a curriculum.

Bill Prescott discusses a cascade model for in-service training, introduced by the Secondary Examinations Council in 1986 which was severely hampered by industrial action. The novelty of the approach – at least in England, Wales and Northern Ireland – none the less justifies attention. Prescott suggests that even had the programme as planned been achieved, its shortcomings, principally stemming from its time-scale, would still have been exposed. John Scarth's contribution has bearing on the, perhaps cynical, view that teachers fall in with a common set of assumptions about the requirements of a syllabus. This important idea has been surprisingly under-researched in the past. Scarth's work suggests that teachers are quite resistant to the exigencies of national initiatives. Taking the example of the Schools Council History Project, he suggests that 'ultimately it is the teacher in relative isolation of the classroom who makes effective decisions about the curriculum'. This would not only cast doubt on the ability of government to introduce change but is in some opposition to earlier contributions, and suggests that teacher autonomy is far from dead. Harry Torrance wants neither centralization nor the form of teacher autonomy described by Scarth. He suggests that lasting, relevant change is best achieved by teachers acting in concert to resolve the dilemmas they face in schools. He fears that the GCSE and the style of in-service provision associated with it, has stultified some of the more promising efforts of teachers to introduce new curricula and, with them, new modes of assessment and certification.

The final section of the book provides perspectives, sometimes necessarily speculatively, on curricular and assessment issues that cannot, or should not, be disassociated from the GCSE reforms. Ian McNay sees the GCSE as a disappointing anachronism that is not only out of step with students' needs but also acting counter to more positive developments such as TVEI and CPVE. In his criticism, McNay argues that the GCSE fails to answer the irresistable call for improving pre-vocational work in schools. He argues, in effect, that the GCSE is a potential blind alley for those seeking full comprehensive education. The reminder that the target group for the GCSE syllabuses, in any case, excludes a significant proportion of students, is underlined by Roger Murphy and David Pennycuick, in their discussion of graded assessments. Graded assessments have somewhat separate backgrounds from the GCSE-style assessments, but may share sufficient common ground to hold out some possibilities for unity. Graded tests, like positive assessments, emphasize the idea that attainable targets, using criteria-based considerations, should be set for students. However, stumbling blocks exist too. The assumption that graded tests encourage greater student motivation is still debatable, and the possibility of a marriage between graded tests and the new national criteria is uncertain in many subjects.

SECTION I

VIEWPOINTS

Chapter 1
A CHANGING ROLE FOR EXAMINATION BOARDS?
Roger Murphy (*University of Southampton*)

THE MYSTERY OF THE PAST

The position, role and structure of the public examination boards in England and Wales represent both some of the most significant features of these education systems and at the same time some of the least well understood. There can be very few analyses of secondary schooling in general, and the nature of the curriculum and the way that it is taught in particular, that have not identified public examinations and the boards that administer them as a major influence. Many have recognized the powerful hold that examination syllabuses have had on teaching both in secondary schools and in other parts of the education system as well. Backwash effects are recognized right down into the early years of primary schooling and the links with courses in higher education represent the original rationale for having such examinations which have, of course, up until quite recently been largely controlled by university examination boards.

To accept that examinations are a powerful force influencing the curriculum and the structure and organization of the education system is one thing, but to understand the nature of that relationship is quite another. A key question in such an analysis has always been whether examination boards with their published syllabuses are restricting and holding back curriculum initiatives and changes within schools, or are instead operating as a pioneering force to initiate change and development. The nature of this dilemma is encapsulated in the title of Mortimore and Mortimore's (1984) *Secondary School Examinations: The Helpful Servants not the Dominating Master*. However, given the line of argument within that particular publication, there must have been more than a hint of irony in the choice of the title. The general conclusion, from it and other similar analyses, is that public examinations do, on balance, operate as a powerful conservative force, inhibiting and delaying curriculum change and development. According to authors such as Hargreaves (1982) public examinations have provided one of the greatest obstacles to the development of a suitable and workable comprehensive school curriculum.

Such motive-mongering is dangerous, of course, it may be more profitable to look at some of the *consequences* of this proliferation of examinations, among which I will discover three. First and perhaps most important, what can fairly be called the grammar-school curriculum continued to hold a central and dominant position in the secondary-school curriculum, despite comprehensive re-organisation.   (Hargreaves, 1982, pp. 50–51)

Whereas many have with great conviction laid at the door of the examination boards the blame for most, if not all, that they found to be undesirable or inappropriate about the curriculum of secondary schools, few have gone further to analyse in more detail how examination boards have come to exert this kind of influence. A number of sociologists have written in an illuminating way about the sociology of assessment as far as the wider analysis of the social functions that have been served by public examinations and associated assessment procedures (Broadfoot, 1979, 1984). What their accounts have barely touched has been the analysis of the boards as organizational cultures. Little has been written about the workings of the individual boards, and what has been written has done little to provide any analysis of the internal power structures that have led to distinctive curriculum and assessment policies. Unfortunately most of what has been written about the work of the boards has been produced by staff working for individual boards, and such sources suffer from the public relations motive underlying their production. Apart from such evidence there are, of course, large numbers of teachers who have in various capacities either worked on a part-time basis as examiners for individual boards, or have sat on board committees. Similarly there are others, including the author of this chapter, who have had the experience of working for an examination board and the associated opportunity of viewing the workings of that board from within. What has been sadly lacking, however, has been any systematic and independent account of the workings of even a single board. Each of them undoubtedly represents a distinct culture with different traditions, organizational and power structures, and an associated network of influences. The lack of understanding of these cultures remains a major limitation to any attempt to analyse possible changes that may occur within the boards as they are reorganized and adapt to running the new GCSE examination.

Before moving on to speculate about the possible nature of such changes, it is worth acknowledging the long-standing recognition that there has been of this huge gap in the documented analysis of the British education system.

Whitty (1976) in a rare attempt to both address this problem and its possible causes concluded that,

It is of course, hardly surprising that there has been little research in this area, since even those boards which boast a large measure of teacher participation are notoriously secretive in their operations. Access to their committee structures is generally restricted to 'insiders' whose loyalty to the organisation limits their freedom to discuss their experiences and the administrative procedures of the boards have remained totally impenetrable. (Whitty, 1976, p. 212)

This analysis of the problem hints very strongly at one of the potential difficulties which will undoubtedly continue to restrict the type of research that would be permitted by any individual board. The boards are, and will remain to be under GCSE, competitive commercial organizations. They depend upon their entry fees as the basis for supporting fairly extensive plant and administrative operations. They are openly in competition with each other and are therefore understandably concerned about the image of their activities that is projected to teachers, schools and the wider public.

It would be inappropriate to dwell any further here on the lack of insights that are publicly available about the detailed workings of the present examination boards. It is however of considerable regret that as we move into a new era for the boards, which will undoubtedly have substantial implications for each of them in the way that they are organized and operate, we will have to accept that we have finally lost the opportunity to conduct the type of detailed research investigation that could have provided a lasting record of their former state. The level of understanding of curriculum change and development during the last thirty-five years and beyond will be necessarily diminished.

REGROUPING FOR A NEW ERA

It has been a fundamental principle of the development of the new GCSE examination that its administration would be left in the hands of the former GCE and CSE examination boards. The idea of setting up an entirely new administrative structure, which some have argued would be necessary in order for substantial changes to occur in the nature and operation of the new examination, has never been seriously considered.

In the Waddell Report of 1978 it was argued that the plans were,

[. . .] designed to utilise the considerable resources which the existing boards already devote to examining. These resources include premises and equipment of a kind that will continue to be required and, above all, experienced staff without whom it would not be possible to make the change to a common system and put it into operation on the timescale envisaged. (Waddell Report, 1978, Part 1, p. 19)

This concern to retain the experience and resources of the former examination boards was linked to a concern expressed in the DES's (1982) policy statement that there were 'too many awarding bodies'. Thus, plans were laid for a regrouping of the boards into four groups in England and one in Wales. Each of these groups will have a specific regional responsibility although, in theory, entries will be permitted from outside that region. Every English GCE and CSE board will therefore have become involved in producing arrangements for conducting GCSE examinations with the other boards in its group. The exact nature of these arrangements varies considerably following the DES policy statement which suggested that examining groups should,

[. . .] conduct examinations for the GCSE as consortia of the existing GCE and CSE boards. Boards may decide to merge in the interests of greater efficiency but they would not otherwise lose their separate identity. In administering the GCSE, however, no board would act independently of the group to which it belongs, and no board would be a member of more than one group. (DES, 1982)

In some boards the view has been taken that to follow the spirit of a truly common examination at 16+, it is essential for the GCE and CSE boards to merge so that an examination group can operate as a single entity in conducting the new examination. Other boards have set up much looser arrangements whereby they can retain much of their former identity whilst at the same time collaborating where necessary to run the GCSE.

The former Secretary of State, Sir Keith Joseph, has further complicated the nature of these joint arrangements by suggesting that the former GCE boards should be given the responsibility for the award of grades A to C, while the CSE boards should become responsible for grades D to G (DES, 1985). How such an arrangement can possibly continue to operate in those groups where a high level of collaborative working is envisaged right from the start is difficult to imagine.

Despite all of this, some CSE boards have already merged and the first actual merger between a GCE and a CSE board (the Oxford Delegacy and the Southern Regional Examinations Board) has now taken place. Others are, no doubt, looking seriously at the possibilities and will undoubtedly wish to secure the positions of their existing staff under the new arrangements.

Of course the information that is available about the groupings of boards and the formal arrangements that are being made for joint work provides only a limited insight into the nature and the implications of these newly constituted examination groups. As we have already noted, each individual board has developed its own distinctive characteristics and will be bringing to the new administrative structures a good deal of experience of operating what have, in some circumstances, been markedly different systems. The extent to which such different philosophies may or may not be carried through into the new arrangements will depend on a range of factors. In some cases old procedures will have to be dropped, either because of the guidelines laid down in the national criteria, or because of the requirements of the SEC committees that are approving all GCSE syllabuses. There are, however, quite a number of issues that will not be resolved in this way, and which will depend on the committee and other decision-making structures that are set up within the boards.

One fear that has been voiced, fairly widely, is that the views of the larger and more powerful GCE boards will, on the whole, carry much more weight than those of the CSE boards. In certain aspects of examining, for example in relation to coursework assessment, consortium moderation arrangements, Mode 3 syllabuses across a wide range of subjects, and the assessment of pupils exhibiting a broad range of achievement, the CSE boards may in fact have had more experience. This experience may in some cases be in danger of being lost if, as is feared, the GCE boards carry forward the majority of their own assessment practices into GCSE.

Whether or not this will be the case, it is inevitable that a great deal of speculation is involved at this stage. There has, however, already been enough evidence of some GCSE planning groups being dominated by GCE board staff to suggest that there is more to this fear than may be widely accepted. On the whole, CSE board staff have been used to carrying wide ranging responsibilities across, for example, a number of subject areas or aspects of the administrative process. This has been a consequence of the small size of some of the boards and has led to such staff relying to a great extent on teacher representatives on committees to bring the specialist knowledge that is required in decision-making. In contrast some GCE board staff, particularly in the larger boards, have been given very specialized responsibilities, sometimes in relation to a single subject area. Where such staff have remained in those posts for quite a long period of time, and that is not uncommon in examination boards, they can become very knowledgeable in their specialist area. This can have the effect of making them appear to be very powerful to their committees, their examiners, and to their CSE counterparts. Macintosh (1985) in noting this phenomenon has confirmed that it has 'created problems from time to time in the preparations for GCSE'.

There are other areas where the boards will bring very different traditions and resources to the joint arrangements. The CSE boards have had a much closer working relationship with LEAs and have also ensured that a large part of the membership of their committees was made up of practising teachers. The GCE boards have, on the whole, had much closer links with universities and have in many ways given teachers a much less central role in their planning and examining procedures.

There is, of course, a danger of over-emphasizing such differences and it is certainly the case that some teachers have served on both GCE and CSE board committees simultaneously; there has also been some movement of administrative staff between the two sectors. Nevertheless, all who have been associated with GCE or CSE examining boards, or who have participated in the early stages of GCSE planning, will recognize the potential tensions that exist, and the challenge that will face those who wish to create a new system that truly draws on all parts of the experience of the past.

The CSE boards were established in 1960 following the recommendations of the Beloe Report. One of the major intentions of that reform of the examination system was to provide more scope for these boards to be teacher-controlled. Their regional responsibilities were designed to encourage a closer working relationship with the teachers and schools that they would be serving. Very little emphasis has been placed on this so far in the discussions about GCSE. This time, the desire seems to be to create much more central control of the boards, which must inevitably be likely to diminish the opportunities that will be offered to teachers to participate in the decision-making processes. This phenomenon has been illustrated again and again in the GCSE development work. The most recent example being the dialogue that has been conducted more or less exclusively between the Secondary Examinations Council and the boards over the desirability of the Grade Criteria that have been produced in ten subjects. In such a climate the level of teacher participation in board committees, and in decision-making procedures, becomes a critical issue. So far, the new arrangements show all the signs of leading to diminished teacher involvement due both to the mixing of the very different GCE and CSE board philosophies on this matter, and to the number of teachers who will lose their existing involvement with their local CSE board once the much larger examining groups start to operate their new procedures.

HOW MUCH WILL CHANGE?

The formation of the new examination groups and the demands of the Secondary Examinations Council will undoubtedly cause some changes to occur within the boards. Whether or not these changes will represent a radical shift in the role adopted by public examination boards is less certain. Macintosh (1982, 1985) has painted a fairly gloomy picture of the potential that he sees for change within the boards.

The boards which run the system virtually without exception remain essentially administrative organisations maintaining that they reflect and respond to the curriculum and do not dictate it – curriculum thinking is thus something alien to those who work for them. All boards suffer from progressive arthritis of the procedures and from varying forms of tunnel vision. The boards operate today as they did in 1945 and indeed since their inception. (Macintosh, 1982, p. 13–14)

Thus, if we accept that the boards do only represent administrative mechanisms then there is a need to look elsewhere to see where change might come from. Macintosh, through his involvement in the CSE examination, has worked towards a system of greater teacher control over course construction and pupil assessment. He sees the optimum role for the boards as being external validating and accrediting bodies that could support an essentially school-based system of course development and assessment. He does, however, recognize that, so far, very little change in this direction has been achieved. Despite all of the enthusiasm that surrounded the setting up of the CSE boards, they have developed, according to Macintosh, into a 'pallid imitation of the GCE Boards'.

Offering teachers a greater opportunity to take control of curriculum development and pupils assessment activities always brings with it the complication of the amount of time that needs to be set aside to do such things. Many who worked hard to develop school-based Mode 3 courses in the early days of the CSE examination found to their cost how much time this took up and, in many cases, what little recognition they received for undertaking these additional duties.

The move to GCSE does not represent the type of move away from centrally controlled public examinations for 16-year-olds that has occurred elsewhere in the world. Macintosh's dream of a change similar to that seen in parts of Australia where former examination boards have been transformed into, or replaced by, State Boards of Education with responsibilities for validating and accrediting school-based activities, seems as far away as it has ever been.

The inclusion of elements of coursework assessment within GCSE represents a token gesture in the direction of greater teacher involvement. The real control over what happens will rest even more firmly with central government. Public examinations more than ever before have been recognized as an ideal mechanism for bringing about curriculum control. The boards, which have operated with a good deal of autonomy in the past, are now going to face a constant demand to have all of their syllabuses and assessment procedures monitored and approved by the Secondary Examinations Council. This body which was set up by the Secretary of State, after the abolition of the Schools Council in 1984, with an entirely government nominated membership, has quite unprecedented powers over virtually everything the boards do in relation to GCSE examinations.

One aspect of the increased central control over the boards has been the development of subject-specific, general, and, more recently, draft grade criteria. All GCSE syllabuses have to conform to these national criteria and much time has been spent amending draft GCSE syllabuses in order to secure SEC approval for them.

CONCLUSIONS

The move to the new GCSE examination will not of itself create a big change in the role of the examination boards. As we have noted, there will be increased collaboration between the boards within each of the four examination groups, but the competition between these groups will continue to be strong.

The boards have been viewed as mainly administrative bodies and it can be assumed that the move to GCSE has already, and will continue to place an enormous burden on those administrative mechanisms. Already the increased workload caused by undertaking the development work for the new examination, whilst continuing to run the old examinations, has been added to by the strain of negotiating mergers and other collaborative arrangements between boards within each group.

At a time of falling rolls in secondary schools, with the associated drop in revenue from examination entry fees, some boards are literally fighting for their survival. In some cases this problem has been solved by mergers; in other cases additional activities and income generating interests have been developed and expanded. GCSE will undoubtedly, despite the hopes of Sir Keith Joseph, the former Secretary of State, require substantially increased candidate entry fees in order to continue to support the substantial administrative costs of the boards.

It is unlikely that the new arrangements will offer much encouragement for those who have argued for greater teacher and school involvement in pupil assessment. The new model looks as though it will be just as remote and mysterious to teachers as examination boards have been in the past. The dominance of the GCE boards will ensure a continued strong university influence over what happens, and the creation of the Secondary Examinations Council has introduced an increased element of central control.

In commercial terms GCSE will probably secure the future of the boards for quite a few more years yet, but in educational terms there will be many who will be regretting that a chance to make a more radical change to our public examination system has been missed.

Our understanding of the way that the old GCE and CSE boards have actually operated is sadly limited. One can only hope that the new GCSE examination groups will be prepared to submit to a much greater level of accountability to both central government, which seems determined to secure this, and to their customers, who will continue to be the local education authorities, the users of the results, teachers, parents, schools, and the young people and adults who in the absence of a real alternative will continue to enter for the exams.

REFERENCES

Beloe Report (1960) *Secondary Schools Examinations other than GCE*, HMSO, London
Broadfoot, P. (1979) *Assessment, Schools and Society*, Methuen, London
Broadfoot, P. (1984) *Selection, Certification and Control*, Falmer Press, London
DES (1982) *Examinations at 16+: A Statement of Policy*, HMSO, London
DES (1985) *General Certificate of Secondary Education: A General Introduction*, HMSO, London
Hargreaves, D. (1982) *The Challenge for the Comprehensive School*, Routledge & Kegan Paul, London
Macintosh, H.G. (1982) The prospects for public examinations in England and Wales, *Educational Analysis*, Vol. 4, No. 2, pp. 13–20
Macintosh, H.G. (1985) The politics of examining, *Secondary Heads Association Review*, Vol. 79, No. 247, pp. 935–945
Mortimore, P. and Mortimore, J. (1984) Secondary School Examinations: The Helpful Servants, not the Dominating Master. Bedford Way Papers 18, University of London Institute of Education, London
Waddell Report (1978) *School Examinations*, HMSO, London
Whitty, G. (1976) Teachers and examiners. In G. Whitty and M. Young (1976). *Explorations in the Politics of School Knowledge*, Nafferton Books, Driffield

Chapter 2
THE TEACHER VIEWPOINT
Walter Roy (*Headmaster and GCSE Examining Group Chairman*)

THE BACKGROUND

When the then Secretary of State, Sir Keith Joseph, announced in November 1982 (DES, 1982) that a common system of examinations would replace the separate GCE and CSE examinations, the reactions of the teaching profession ranged from cautious welcome to the reform, to a sense of relief that a decision had been taken. The difficulty of selecting pupils for either the GCE or CSE examination before their fourth year of secondary education, the complexities of two separate grading systems and, above all, the worsening resource crisis in schools which was making it increasingly difficult, and sometimes impossible, to timetable separate teaching groups, indicated very clearly that the dual system was breaking up. The rapid growth in entries for joint O-level/CSE examinations, though still certificated separately, was clear evidence of the way things were going in schools. The reform had been advocated and pioneered by the teaching profession itself, with the National Union of Teachers (NUT) leading the way and consistently advocating a single system throughout the 1970s and early 1980s. A constant stream of publications, (NUT, 1967, 1976a,b,c, 1977, 1978a,b, 1980, 1981a,b, 1983, 1984, Walker, 1977) conference resolutions and speeches by NUT representatives on the Schools Council before its dissolution by Sir Keith Joseph in 1983 indicated the leading role the union was playing. The NUT was powerfully supported by the other major teachers' unions, especially the Assistant Masters' and Mistresses' Association (AMMA) and the National Association of Schoolmasters and Union of Women Teachers (NAS/UWT).

The debate about the proposed reform had lasted some fifteen years: the Schools Council had come out in favour of reform; its successor, the Secondary Examinations Council, although composed largely of the Secretary of State's nominees, had come to the same conclusion, both bodies endorsing the findings of the Waddell Committee, which had reported in 1978, which also advocated a common system. Neither Shirley Williams, as Secretary of State, nor her Conservative successor after the 1979 election, Mark Carlisle, had felt able to make the essential decision to institute the change for which there was massive support in the schools. Sir Keith Joseph, while hesitating for a time and exploring the harmonization of the dual system, finally ruled in favour of radical reform. It looked as if the teachers, who after all knew what examining was all about, had won the day. The NUT, critical of nearly all Sir Keith's policies, welcomed his decision; for a short while, the adversaries were on the same side.

But was it the common system which the teachers wanted? Was it really the radical reform envisaged and needed, or had some old wine been poured into new bottles to make the reform look attractive, and yet maintain as much separatism as possible within the common system?

Some reservations about the nature and extent of the reform were already evident before the Secretary of State's announcement, and these gained momentum as the nature of the change penetrated the schools. Four distinct but interrelated attitudes emerged among teachers. First, there were serious professional reservations about the application of national criteria. Next, there were deep-seated philosophical differences between the way the Secretary of State saw the changes operating and the manner in which the teaching profession looked upon the whole philosophy of examining. Third, there were clear political differences, and last, but not least, there were practical considerations about the time-scale for making the change. It was clear that major problems were likely to be encountered unless some of the differences were resolved and the reservations overcome.

APPLYING THE NATIONAL CRITERIA

Teachers had known for some years that a price had to be paid for the introduction of the GCSE and the abolition of the GCE and CSE. The price was the virtual abandonment of their freedom to shape syllabuses, the disappearance of assessment procedures largely based on teachers' professional judgement and the acceptance of a set of ground rules, known as national criteria, decided by the Department of Education and Science. The heyday of the early 1960s which followed the publication of the Beloe Report (1960) and the introduction of the CSE was over. At that time the schools were the masters and the Examination Boards the servants. The CSE, by introducing continuous assessment on a large scale, often coexisting with the usual written papers, but sometimes replacing them, the growth of oral examining, the abandonment of the pass/fail concept and, above all, the control of the CSE Examination Boards by the teachers were vital professional gains now under threat. By the early 1980s, however, a different climate existed in which central government wanted more and more say in how both schools and examinations were run. Such intervention was unwelcome to the teachers and their unions; nevertheless, they entered into the debate about the shaping of the national criteria with a sense of realism and cooperated with the Secretary of State by participating in the work of the Joint Council for National Criteria, which completed its task of publishing subject-specific criteria by April 1985.

Once the task of syllabus construction began in earnest in the joint subject panels of the GCE and CSE boards, the true nature of the national criteria became apparent: the twenty subject-specific criteria published by 1985 (DES, 1985) showed considerable variation in content, approach and philosophy. The criteria for English, mathematics, biology, chemistry, physics, computer studies, French, craft, design and technology, music and classical subjects were roughly equal in length and had a similar approach. However, those for science and home economics went into considerably more detail and were three times as long. Religious studies, business studies, art and design, geography and history were dealt with in considerably less detail, taking up only half-a-dozen pages, and economics and social science were despatched in a mere three pages, as if the drafters had run out of energy or time. Such variations were significant because they reflected the essential diversity of approach in a system geared towards greater uniformity. The controversy about the criteria for home economics was illustrative of the difficulty. The Secretary of State required that the themes of family, food, home and textiles should feature in all syllabuses, and this led to immediate difficulties. In most schools, home economics existed as a separate subject from child development and textiles, and the wide syllabus envisaged would have required at least double the current teaching time. Both subject teachers, and school heads, opposed DES intervention. Eventually a compromise was struck, making it possible to develop separate syllabuses. Time and energy could have been saved if matters had been left more flexible: the teachers knew what they were about; it is doubtful whether the Secretary of State did.

THE PHILOSOPHY OF ASSESSMENT

But there were other problems besides those relating to matters of content and approach. Many teachers had even greater reservations about the proposed assessment procedures, and in particular disliked the insistence on differentiation which permeated both general and nearly all the subject-specific criteria. Although there was a concession in the general criteria that in many subjects, a mixture of common and differentiated arrangements would be appropriate (DES, 1985), the emphasis throughout was on a heavily differentiated system, which led to detailed instructions when the subject-specific criteria were related to the seven-point grading system (to be discussed later). This rigidity of approach caused dismay in many schools, where the option system had frequently led to teaching groups based on interest rather than ability. While setting was common in English, mathematics, modern languages and some sciences, in many other subjects schools either had a deliberate policy of mixed-ability teaching for fourth and fifth year groups, or had been forced into such a policy because they could not afford to timetable differentiated groups for GCE and CSE examinations. Such resource problems had played their part in the tremendous growth in entries for the carefully devised joint O-level/CSE examinations which had existed, and operated successfully, without national criteria. Many teachers feared that the common objectives of the GCSE might become submerged in the need to satisfy the differentiated criteria, if these were applied rigidly, and early responses from the Secondary Examinations Council's subject panels seemed to indicate that rigid application of the criteria was likely.

Such comments must be taken seriously, but in no way lessen the profession's continuing support for the introduction of the GCSE. The syllabus is the teachers' major operational tool, determining not only what is taught but also the method of teaching. If can offer at one and the same time, a stimulus of educational advancement and a refuge for conformity. One of the great criticisms levelled against the GCE examination, sometimes unfairly, related to the restrictive nature of the syllabuses, whereas the CSE was often seen as a liberating force. Many of the notions of the CSE have been built into the general criteria and yet, although the ground rules appear sensible and well thought out, the subject-specific criteria often err towards rigidity and conformism.

Yet another matter of deep concern relates to the introduction of the seven-point grading system and the way it is to be applied. The five-point scale operating in both the GCE (grades A, B, C, D, E) and the CSE (grades 1, 2, 3, 4, 5), with ungraded performances recorded on the results slip, was widely accepted as providing sufficient differentiation in certification for employers, higher and further education interests, and for parents. Yet the new system provides a complex seven-point scale (A, B, C, D, E, F, G), with the ungraded performances retained, and grade F geared towards the performance of the average candidate. The notion that candidates should be examined on the basis of what they know rather than what they do not know, widely welcomed by teachers and rooted in the philosophy of the CSE in its abolition of the pass/fail concept, could have been applied purposefully in a five-point grading scheme. The NUT advocated this in its submission to the Waddell Committee (Waddell Report, 1980) and there was a wide professional consensus on this point. The teachers were sharply critical of a grading system which envisages a substantial proportion of the school population obtaining grades F or G; the risk of examinees becoming disenchanted once the significance of this change is fully appreciated should not be underestimated. Pressure is likely to build up in the next few years to modify the grading system and return to a five-point scale.

The requirement that O-level boards are to be responsible for maintainng standards for grades A to C, while CSE boards are to exercise corresponding responsibility for grades D to G, has not been well received by the teachers who actually do the work. Subject panels for the GCSE are composed of representatives from both sets of boards; they work together as one team and look at the totality of the examining process. Where joint schemes have been in operation for many years, e.g. in the joint CSE/O-level examinations pioneered by the East Anglian CSE Board and the Cambridge Local Examinations Syndicate, such differences are considered both artificial and unnecessary. The sooner such barriers are removed, the better.

Taking all these issues together, and studying the reactions of the major teachers' organizations, and of the many teachers serving on subject panels, committees and councils of the boards, the gap in philosophy between what the government and what the profession sees as the needs of the pupils, becomes apparent. The teachers see the new examination as an essential component in a unified secondary school system which has had to suffer the disadvantages of separatism in examining at 16+. Too rigid an insistence on national criteria, whether general or subject-specific, too heavy an emphasis on differentiation in assessment procedures, too fine a grading system, and the possible introduction of distinction and merit certificates, look like attempts to preserve considerable elements of selection within a common system.

THE POLITICAL CONTEXT

There are differences not only of philosophy, but also of politics. In a highly charged political atmosphere with the government and the teachers' unions both engaged in a bruising struggle over salaries, the risk that confrontation and antagonisms will spill into the examinations sphere, are considerable: in 1985, both the NUT and the NAS/UWT have asked their members not to participate in developmental work on GCSE although the NUT wants members to continue to play a political role while the system is under discussion. In addition, the profession continues to protest at the increasingly interventionist stance of the Department of Education and Science in the day to day affairs of the schools. One pronouncement follows another, often in rapid succession, on all aspects of the curriculum. The assumption, by government, that it is entitled to direct and control curricular movements is both resented and resisted. The existence of some 4000 Mode 3 syllabuses most of which have been designed by individual teachers, tailored to the needs of the pupils in their localities, is a powerful reminder that examining is not seen as the business of central government.

RESOURCING THE NEW EXAM

Another major aspect of the debate relates to the provision of resources necessary to introduce the new system. This has several dimensions. First and foremost, there is the desperate need to find time to implement the change. The initial in-service training provided has been seen as inadequate both by the professional associations and certainly by the majority of secondary school teachers. The training of some 60 000 team leaders, usually heads of subject departments, for two days a week, in no way ensured that the knowledge they gained would be passed on to members of their departments.

The resource crisis is likely to become worse as schools begin to teach the new syllabuses. Although some syllabuses have been designed with considerable sensitivity, taking account of the requirement stated in the General Criteria 'that the syllabus and particularly the scheme of assessment, must not make unreasonable demands on human and financial resources' (DES, 1985), there can be no doubt that new syllabuses require new teaching materials. Textbooks, readers, equipment, apparatus and files are only some of the items which are needed by hard-pressed and under-resourced subject departments. Although many CSE syllabuses contained continuous assessment procedures, often in the form of marking projects compiled during the fourth and fifth years, the bulk of examining was still on the basis of timed papers at the end of the course. And this was almost universally the case with the GCE examination. The integration of continuous assessment in new schemes of work and the marking of such work in accordance with grade-related criteria, represent not only a considerable increase in workload, but also in responsibility. The same is true of the spread of oral examining. To examine every candidate in every school in oral English is no mean undertaking, and requires large scale rearrangements of timetables and examination procedures. The climate is vastly different from that which pertained when CSE got off the ground, twenty years ago. No such climate exists today nor is it likely to exist in the near future. This is not to suggest that the profession does not want the changes; on the contrary, continuous assessment and the spread of oral examining are favoured by practically every teacher. But the commitment to progressive methods of examining which underpin the reform does not extend to giving hours and hours of unpaid time when they feel that the government is hostile to them, and when teacher assessment looms on the horizon and is seen as a threat by many of them. These harsh realities could pose a threat to the successful introduction of GCSE. This threat can be lessened, and even removed by a genuine change of stance by those who have their hands on the lever of power: what is needed are a new pay settlement, positive pronouncements to encourage the profession, an appreciation of the difficulties teachers face in the eighties, and above all, the provision of additional resources both for school and local education authorities.

CONTROLLING EXAMINATIONS

The attitudes individual teachers and teachers' unions have towards the management, and in particular, the government of the examining bodies, are significant factors. Four new examining groups, the Midland Group, the London East Anglian Group, the Northern Examining Association and the Southern Group, each containing both the GCE and CSE boards in their respective areas, are getting off the ground in a purposeful and positive way. Although some constitutional problems remain to be ironed out, there is no doubt that teacher influence will be significant in the new group governing councils.

Two models are emerging, one favouring a unitary, the other a federal approach. The Midland Examining Group makes specific provision for seventeen representatives drawn from teachers' associations to serve on its governing council. The federal model ensures the presence of teachers on the governing councils both through the elected representatives of the separate boards, and through the allocation of a number of seats to each union. Below that level, various examination, coordinating, and management committees have significant numbers of teachers. These are healthy signs and suggest that the teaching profession is aware of the need to maintain a powerful presence in the Examination Groups and associated bodies. The constitutions which have emerged are not dissimilar to that of the dissolved Schools Council in which teacher union representatives, LEA spokesmen, employers, parents, representatives of higher education interests the Inspectorate, and the DES, all participated, giving the Council the character of an educational parliament. The SEC contains no representatives of teachers' unions, and there are few teachers present at Council meetings; the SEC is the poorer for it. The formation, in May 1985, of a new council of GCE and CSE boards (Joint Council for GCSE, 1985) illustrates the independence of the Examination Groups from the SEC and the DES. This council certainly regards itself as a spokesman for the examination fraternity and provides a platform for well-known teacher spokesmen from the examining world. This is as it should be; it is after all, the teachers in the schools and the classrooms who have to live with the decisions made at the highest levels in the examinations world. The system of public examinations is deeply rooted in schools and colleges and has shown a flexibility and adaptability over the years which makes it likely that it will continue for some time. The teachers, given the tools to operate the GCSE, will do the job.

REFERENCES

Beloe Report (1960) *Secondary Schools Examination other than GCE*, HMSO, London
DES (1982) *Examinations at 16+: A Statement of Policy*, HMSO, London
DES (1985) *GCSE – The General Certificate of Secondary Education – the National Criteria*, HMSO, London
LEAG (1985a) *GCSE In-Service Training News*, London and East Anglian Group for GCSE, London
LEAG (1985b) *General Criteria*, London and East Anglian Group for GCSE, London
NUT (1967) *Examining at 16+*, NUT, London
NUT (1976a) *Examinations at 16+ — Proposals for the Future*, NUT, London
NUT (1976b) *Examinations at 16+ — Proposals for the Future: A Policy Statement*, NUT, London
NUT (1976c) *Discussion Document on 'Examinations at 16+ — Proposals for the Future'*, NUT, London
NUT (1977) *Examinations at 16+ and 17+*, NUT conference, London, 16 March
NUT (1978a) *Examining at 16+ — the Case for a Common System*, NUT, London
NUT (1978b) *Examining at 16+ — an NUT Policy Statement*, NUT, London
NUT (1980) *Examining at 16+ — an NUT Policy Statement on Proposals for a Single System*, NUT, London
NUT (1981a) *A Single System of Examining at 16+: National Criteria*, NUT, London
NUT (1981b) *Curriculum and Examinations: Memorandum of Evidence Submitted by the NUT to the Education, Science and Arts Committee in Curriculum and Examinations for the 14–16 Age Group*, NUT, London
NUT (1983) *Examining at 16+ — a Policy Statement by the NUT*, NUT, London
NUT (1984) *A Single System of Examination at 16+: Key Educational Issues*, NUT, London

Walker, D. (1977) A guide to examinations. Paper presented to the NUT Conference on Examinations at 16+ and 17+, London, 16 March
Waddell Report (1978) *School Examinations*, HMSO, London

Chapter 3
THE DEPARTMENT OF EDUCATION AND SCIENCE – STEERING A NEW COURSE
Brian Salter (*University of Surrey*) and Ted Tapper (*University of Sussex*)

INTRODUCTION

Suddenly, the pace of educational change is quickening as the Department of Education and Science shrugs off the pretence of consensus management. After years of patient diplomacy, of prodding and nudging, of two steps forward and one step back, the DES is now in the position of being able unreservedly to state and, to an extent, implement its centralizing ambitions. Secondary examinations are one arena in which this is happening. Others are teacher training, the DES–LEA relationship, and higher education. In this chapter we explore how, in the case of the GCSE, the Department has arrived in this position.

Although part of the answer to this question undoubtedly lies in the nature of what we have called the Department's 'bureaucratic dynamic' with its impetus towards more management controls over the education system (Salter and Tapper, 1981), part of it lies outside the DES in that network of intellectuals and institutions which has sponsored the New Right's ideas on education (Salter and Tapper, 1985). It is our argument that these two influences have come together to produce what appears to be an unstoppable momentum towards greater state control in education.

A WAITING GAME

The DES is not interested in the control of secondary examinations *per se* but in the fact that examinations determine the nature of the curriculum. Its interest in curriculum control goes back a long way. In 1962, the Curriculum Study Group was set up within the then Ministry of Education with the brief of commissioning research and making recommendations in the fields of curriculum and examinations. It followed the urging of Sir David Eccles, Minister of Education, that 'the secret garden of the curriculum', as he termed it, should no longer remain immune from government influence. However, such was the opposition to this move that it was abandoned, and in 1963, the teacher-dominated Schools Council for Curriculum and Examinations, independent of the DES, was created in its stead. The Schools Council also took on board the functions of the old Secondary Schools Examination Council (SSEC) with regard to O- and A- levels. Round one to the teaching profession.

The response of the DES to the birth of this unwanted child was one of reluctant toleration coupled with a determination to give as little practical assistance as possible until the opportunity should arise to remove it. In any case, at that stage the bureaucratic pressures within the Department for an expansion of its managerial controls over education were only just beginning to emerge. Furthermore, the left-progressive ideas which dominated educational thought in Britain in the 1960s and early 1970s were highly unsympathetic to any central intervention in the curriculum. Characterized by a child-centred approach to teaching, informal pedagogic and assessment methods, and an antipathy to inequality and hierarchy, progressive education naturally favoured a decentralized system of education with the classroom teacher as the prime mover of events. So long as these ideas held sway it was extremely difficult for the DES to gather any general political support for its interventionist ambitions, regardless of how modest these might be. Even the Schools Council, controlled though it was by authentic teachers, was obliged to tread warily within this climate of opinion. Its constitution was at pains to stress its advisory role: it could 'offer advice *on request* to schools' but,

[. . .] regard shall at all times be had to the general principle that each school should have the fullest possible measure of responsibility for its own work, with its own curriculum and teaching methods based on the needs of its own pupils and evolved by its own staff. (Schools Council, 1978, paras. 36, 13, 14)

While the idea of school autonomy retained the power embodied in this statement, any attempt at central control would be dismissed as illegitimate.

Ideological change is therefore a necessary precursor of organizational change and ideological conflict is a sure sign that someone is trying to alter the existing distribution of power. If the DES was to make any inroads into the school curriculum it had first to shunt the left-progressive ideology into the sidings. For reasons which we shall discuss shortly, an ideological offensive by the DES was not possible until the mid-1970s. Until then, the Department had to grin and bear it.

Given the teaching profession's dominance of the Schools Council, the DES was always unlikely to cooperate with its proposals on examinations since this would simply serve to endorse and legitimize the right of the Council to make such proposals. Cooperation would only further entrench the body whose functions the DES wanted for itself and, as a result, help to perpetuate teacher power over the curriculum. Not surprisingly, therefore, the history of the Schools Council on examinations is littered with examples of recommendations rejected by the DES after suitably lengthy discussion. Up to 1983 when it was dissolved, the only Council proposal on examinations accepted by the Secretary of State was the A, B, C, D system of grading at O-level. Of the others, the government rejected the recommendations for twenty-point grading of A-levels in 1972, and the proposals to replace A-levels with N and F-levels in 1979. In the case of the Council's proposals on a common system of examining at 16+, and on the Certificate for Extended Education (CEE), the DES employed the working party tactic as a delaying device until the Council could be abolished. (The 16+ proposals were examined by a working party under the chairmanship of Sir James Waddell and the CEE proposals by a study-group chaired by Professor Keohane.)

At the same time as this holding operation was in progress, the New Right prepared to seize the ideological initiative with the publication of the first *Black Paper* in 1969. It was inevitable that, at first, those who challenged the left-progressive consensus in education should be dismissed as cranks and eccentrics: any ideological hegemony will try to emasculate emergent opposition in this way. But by 1971, 80 000 copies of the first three *Black Papers* had been sold and the challenge was on the move. Organizations such as the Institute for Economic Affairs, the National Council for Educational Standards and the Centre for Policy Studies added their weight to the movement and slowly but surely the credibility of its ideas increased.

The New Right was under no illusions about the task that faced it in seeking to change the dominant climate of opinion in education. It saw itself as taking on what it called 'the progressive establishment' composed of the DES, Her Majesty's Inspectorate (HMI), the teachers' unions, and sometimes, though not always, the local education authorities. It was among the ranks of education's officialdom that the New Right saw the progressive ideology as most securely bedded. The officials in turn were aided and abetted by likeminded members of academia and the media who propagated and legitimized the progressive establishment's line.

In the light of the New Right's analysis of its political opposition, an alliance between itself and the DES seemed, to say the least, a little unlikely even assuming it was wrong about the Department's commitment to progressive education. To understand the reasons for this alliance we need briefly to describe the New Right's ideas on education. The principal aim is the improvement of the quality of the educational experience. Clearly the New Right has a particular understanding of what quality in education means in terms of traditional moral and cultural values, knowledge areas and teaching methods. If this educational quality is to be achieved, two conditions have to be fulfilled. Firstly, there has to be common and explicit agreement on the definition of quality in education in order that people have a goal to work towards: in other words there have to be national standards in education. Secondly, there has to be a mechanism for implementing and monitoring these standards. The natural preference of the New Right is for the operation of parental choice in the educational market to force up standards. If parents are given the ability, and the information, to choose between schools, it is argued, then schools will have to compete for their business by improving the quality of the service on offer. Quality is here assumed to be indicated by examination results and herein lies a problem.

As independent, self-financing bodies, the examination boards for CSE, O- and A-levels compete for business from the schools. The quality of the qualification offered by the different boards has, up to now, almost certainly varied from board to board. This is because although there have been national qualifications in secondary education there have been no national criteria which could be applied equally and impartially to each qualification. Thus neither the examination boards nor the public have been in the position to judge the quality of a qualification according to known and commonly accepted criteria. If parents are to choose a school on the basis of the quality of its exam results then clearly such national examination criteria must be established.

The logic of the New Right's ideology means that it shares a common cause with the DES in three areas: the concern to make what goes on in the classroom accountable to an external authority; the need to establish national standards by which to judge a school's achievements; and, as a consequence of these first two, the desire to reduce the autonomy and power of the teaching profession. Adeptly employed, it therefore has the capacity to legitimize DES intervention in the curriculum.

GOING FOR IT

That the upper echelons of the DES were fully aware of the importance of ideology to their bid for greater bureaucratic power is clearly shown by the

Yellow Book, an internal DES document carefully leaked in September 1976 (TES, 1976). The Yellow Book argued for an authoritative pronouce-ment from the Prime Minister which would both suggest that the Depart-ment should give a firmer lead on what goes on in schools and refute the argument that no one except teachers has any right to such a say. It concluded:

The *climate for such a declaration* on these lines may in fact now be relatively favourable. Nor need there be any inhibitions for fear that the Department could not make use of enhanced opportunity to exercise influence over curriculum and teaching methods. (*Times Educational Supplement*, 1976, emphasis added)

The fact that such a climate of opinion existed in 1976, when it had not existed ten years earlier, and that Callaghan felt compelled to make his speech at Ruskin College, Oxford, in October of that year in response to the changing public view of education, are tributes to the campaign waged by the New Right. The left-progressive consensus in education was under siege and the opportunity for the DES to make a clear bid for power had arrived.

In ideological terms, the preference of the Department is for what we have termed the 'economic ideology of education' which sees education as serving the economic needs of the nation. Central intervention by the DES is then presented as enabling the education system to provide that service more effectively and more efficiently (Tapper and Salter, 1978, Chapter 7). On its own, it was unlikely that the Department could successfully mount an ideological challenge to the left-progressive hegemony. But when the impact on that hegemony of the New Right was added to the political equation, the future for the DES looked considerably brighter.

The 'great debate' on education which followed Callaghan's Ruskin College speech was designed to provide the ideological platform for greater state intervention. Initiated and controlled by the DES, it took full advan-tage of the cracks in the left-progressive facade caused by New Right pressure. It constantly emphasized the themes of core curriculum, basic literacy and numeracy, the monitoring of standards, improving the quality of teacher training and the accountability of education to the community – all of which are consistent with the ideological positions of both the New Right and the DES.

A clear indication of the influence of the New Right on the debate was the publication of the Taylor Report on school government in September 1977. The report sought to take power away from teachers and put it in the hands of school governors composed of school staff, LEA representatives, parents and local community representatives. The gap between the reactions of the teachers' unions to this novel idea at the time and the climate of opinion today illustrates how far the public view of education has shifted since 1977. Fred Jarvis of the NUT called it a 'busybodies' charter' (Vaughan, 1977) and asserted that 'there are points at which the teacher as a professional has to tell the layman that it is his job to know and to decide' (Cohen and Lodge, 1977). Likewise the NAS/UWT said the report offered 'a "bogus" partnership' because it was impossible for lay people 'intelligently to share in the management of the education system' (Vaughan, 1977)! Times have certainly changed.

Having helped establish an ideological context in which increased central management in education is regarded as not only legitimate but also necessary, the DES then faced the problem of how to develop the required lines of administrative control over the curriculum. Despite regular prodding with government circulars, the bodies with the legal responsibility for the school curriculum, the LEAs, have shown themselves remarkably resistant to developing the curricular policies requested of them by the DES. And given the Department of the Environment's control over the allocation of local authority finance coupled with local authority discretion on how it is spent, the DES is not in the position of being able to operate any real financial sanctions over LEA failure to meet educational targets. One way around this has been to shift the role of HMI away from an advisory function towards a monitoring function in terms of the information it collects, the values it propagates, and the criteria it applies. Another has been the DES's much closer interest in the quality of teacher training and the emergent role of the Council for the Accreditation of Teacher Education. A third has been to use the development of the GCSE examination as a vehicle for establishing DES control over the examination system in secondary schooling.

ADMINISTRATIVE GAME PLAY

Having removed the irritant of the Schools Council from the political arena in April 1982 the Department announced that two bodies would replace it: the Secondary Examinations Council (SEC) and the School Curriculum Development Committee (SCDC). The organization and composition of the two bodies stand in sharp contrast to that of the old Schools Council and illustrate how, in this field at least, the power of the teachers' unions has been stripped away. The SEC is financed by the Department and its members are personally appointed by the Secretary of State. The SCDC is funded jointly by the DES and the LEAs and the responsibility for the appointment of its members divided between the two.

It is the responsibility of the SEC 'to coordinate and seek to improve the school examination system and other forms of school-based assessment in England and Wales, and it is the source of advice to the government on these areas of policy' (DES, 1983, p. 9). If the SEC is to coordinate the examination system effectively then it is inevitable that the exam boards will have to relinquish some of their cherished independence and powers. Why should they do so? Legally, the SEC is a company limited by guarantee which is also a registered charity and has no statutory power to force the exam boards to do anything.

Its informal power derives from the need of the exam boards and the Secretary of State for a body which will facilitate the change to a common system of examining at 16+. The Joint Council of GCE and CSE Boards could take the first step of developing subject-specific national criteria but was not able, or was not allowed, to have the authority to carry out the coordinating functions of appraising the national criteria, monitoring syllabuses and assessment procedures adopted by Examining Groups, and monitoring the conduct of GCSE examinations and comparability of standards. Once the exam boards had accepted the authority of the SEC to discharge these functions, they were then rapidly drawn into a bureaucratic web of committees, spun with consummate skill by the DES, from which there was little chance of escape. The addition of grade related criteria to the SEC's shopping list then added a further bureaucratic layer of activities and sealed the fate of the exam boards completely.

One wonders how the protagonists of the New Right view this expansion of the central state's controls in education. On the one hand, explicit national standards are necessary if improvements in the quality of education are to be seen to be achieved. For example, if Sir Keith Joseph's ambition stated in his 1984 Sheffield speech of bringing 80–90 percent of all pupils at least to the level associated with CSE grade 4 is to be achieved, then that standard has to be precisely defined. On the other hand, once the SEC has completed its task of defining national standards in the form of grade related criteria for each subject, presumably supporters of the New Right would wish it to be disbanded and the maintenance of standards left to the market mechanism of parental choice. Obviously the DES will fight tooth and nail to ensure that no such action is taken and that the SEC remains part of the state apparatus.

The advantages to both the DES and the New Right of an alliance which keeps left-progressive values and policies out of the educational mainstream are such that both sides will want to preserve it. In his Sheffield speech, Sir Keith Joseph outlined a number of stepping stones on the way to raising the standards of performance in schools:

[. . .] the establishment of an accreditation council for initial teacher training; the decision on the future shape of the 16+ examination system based on national criteria; the formation of a curricular policy in each LEA for pupils of all abilities and aptitudes – Circular 8/83; a definitive statement on the objectives of science in schools; a start on the formulation of grade-related criteria for the 16+ examinations; and the definition of a scheme of pilot projects on records of achievement for all school leavers. (SEC, 1984, p. 68)

The issue of standards has been a New Right rallying call since the first *Black Paper*. Giving it administrative reality in the ways listed by Sir Keith suits the DES very well indeed. The GCSE and the development of the SEC is no doubt a particularly pleasing experience of postponed bureaucratic gratification for the DES. It has, after all, been waiting such a long time to enter the secret garden.

REFERENCES

Cohen, S. and Lodge, B. (1977) 'Blundering intruders' warned (report of Jarvis's speech to NUT Conference), *Times Educational Supplement*, 15 April, p. 6

DES (1983) *Annual Report 1983*, HMSO, London

Salter, B. and Tapper, T. (1981) *Education, Politics and the State: The Theory and Practice of Educational Change*, Grant McIntyre, London

Salter, B. and Tapper, T. (1985) *Power and Policy in Education: The Case of Independent Schooling*, Falmer Press, London

Schools Council (1978) Constitution of the Schools Council for Curriculum and Examinations, London, *Schools Council Report*, Evans/Methuen, London

Secondary Examinations Council (1984) *Annual Report 1983–84*, Secondary Examinations Council, London

Tapper, T. and Salter, B. (1978) *Education and the Political Order: Changing Patterns of Class Control*, Macmillan Press, London

Times Educational Supplement (1976) Extracts from the Yellow Book, 15 October, pp. 2–3

Vaughan, M. (1977) Snub for 'busybodies' charter, *Times Educational Supplement*, 23 September, p. 1

Chapter 4
TOWARDS A CONSERVATIVE CURRICULUM?
Peter Scrimshaw (*Open University*)

The dominant feature of Conservative governments in the 1980s has been a commitment to a superficially conceived rationalism, to managerialism, and to the removal of foci for opposition to centralized state control. None of these features is intrinsically linked with Conservatism as it has been historically understood in Britain, and where more traditional Tory values have been incompatible with the new ideology it has been the traditional values that have gone under. The GCSE is one attempt by the government to implement this new ideology. Responses to the new system will have to recognize this if they are to be effective, and this paper attempts to identify some of the main issues that have to be addressed by supporters and critics of the GCSE alike.

Considered as an exercise in curriculum control the GCSE can be usefully viewed from three perspectives. First, the criteria and assessment regulations specify, more or less precisely, what content and aims are permitted. Second, the new system redistributes control over the examination system, and thus over the curriculum. Finally there is the question of the possible directions in which the GCSE might develop in the future.

Some critics of the new system see the GCSE as perpetuating a traditional single-subject curriculum, as against one that encourages integration. To the extent that the criteria do not include integrated titles, such as humanities or integrated studies, this is true. On the other hand, several of the sets of national criteria (such as those for craft, design and technology, classical subjects, home economics, and art and design) promote varying degrees of integration within a range of curriculum areas. The GCSE follows the rather slow contemporary trend towards greater integration, even if it shows few signs of leading it. However, the relationship between criteria and examination subjects is complex and shows wide divergences. At one extreme, there are straightforward matches between a set of criteria and a traditional subject, such as mathematics. In the case of English language and literature there are separate requirements which both echo and challenge the distinction between the two. The classical subjects criteria document names seven subjects that it is intended to cover; the art and design document names none. Business studies specifies only that it does not apply to subjects such as commerce. The role the criteria play in redefining the relationships between the subjects they cover varies greatly from one part of the curriculum to another.

Schools currently have different patterns of subjects from those in the criteria documents. In classical studies, for instance, few school timetables will have three or four subjects covered by the national criteria, so that the question of the relationship between such subjects is not raised by the GCSE debate. In the case of craft, design and technology, however, there may well be several examination subjects in a school that fall under the criteria. Where this is so, the presentation and discussion of the criteria, and far more the choice of examination syllabuses may become the focus for structural change within the school's curriculum, and possibly in the school's departmental organization too. This picture of diversity is somewhat tempered when we examine the aims, objectives and content presented within the different documents. The criteria define aims, assessment objectives, core content and the relationship between objectives and assessment techniques. While this shared framework is a strong feature in all the documents, there are still very important variations between them.

The distinction drawn in the General Criteria between desirable aims and assessable objectives is common to all subjects but a range of methods are used to conceptualize aims, objectives, content and their relationships. First, there are wide divergencies in the detail in which objectives and content are specified. To take one crude indicator of this, the Welsh criteria include some twenty objectives, whereas the English language objectives number only eight. Similarly, no content is specified as compulsory for history, although a satisfactory understanding of geography is felt to require coverage of five content areas, and biology specifies some twenty content areas as compulsory. All religious studies syllabuses must select their content from six (specified) religions, but may be based upon the study of any one, two or three of them. Each Examining Group is obliged to provide at least one syllabus in which Christianity is the sole religion studied.

On the face of it, the more detailed the specification of a subject's objectives, the more tightly will teachers be constrained by them and the less room there will be for diversity within the subject. But the pressure for conformity in a given subject is also affected by the relationship between assessment on the one hand and objectives and content on the other. Here too, there are considerable variations, as the following four examples illustrate.

In Welsh, the twenty objectives listed are divided into three categories, each carrying equal marks. This ensures tight control of the mark allocation at the general level, but considerable flexibility in how marks are allocated between specific objectives.

Social science examinations must divide marks between four categories: recall, organization, analysis and interpretation/evaluation/application. How these relate to the six objectives specified is not immediately clear, especially as objective 3.4 requires that the candidates demonstrate 'the abilities to recall, organize, analyse, interpret and evaluate social scientific knowledge and apply that knowledge.' What is clear is that the Examining Boards are allowed to vary the mark allocations between the four categories by a factor of 1.5 to 2.0. This then offers a much greater range of acceptable weightings than in the case of Welsh, and at the same time allows examinations to be so structured as to make it hard to judge how well groups of students or candidates for a particular examination have done in relation to any specific assessment objective laid down in the national criteria.

The economics document also defines no close relationship between its five objectives and its two assessment categories. Thus knowledge and understanding can be allocated up to 40 per cent of the marks, while application of knowledge, analysis and judgement must be given a minimum of 60 per cent. This formulation is quite compatible with allocating 100 per cent of marks to the second category and none at all to the first.

By contrast, the chemistry examination is highly detailed in its mark allocations. Using a complex 4 × 4 grid of objectives and content, it sets minimum percentages for marks for the content areas, requires the addition of a third of the total marks for extensions to the core content, and then sets requirements for the percentages to be allocated for each of the objectives categories too. How much room for independent judgement this structure actually allows Examining Boards is not immediately apparent, especially as the criteria include very detailed notes on what is called 'a possible amplification of the core' for each of the thirty to forty content elements specified in the compulsory core. Whether 'possible' in this context means 'the only possible extension for this element if you wish to extend it' or 'one possible example of the sort of extension you might decide to include' is unclear. Here, as at many other points, the national criteria are by no means self-explanatory.

As they stand, the national criteria represent only a partially successful attempt to provide a set of comparable frameworks for a very diverse range of subjects. Nevertheless, the existence of the criteria will reduce the range of kinds of examination available. This is because prohibitive rules by their nature exclude possibilities. They can reduce diversity, but they cannot create it where it does not exist. Their effect therefore will be to eliminate some of the present kinds of examination. The scale of the reduction remains to be seen, and will no doubt vary from one subject area to another. However, it may be that the real choices open to schools, as distinct from the apparent ones, are actually increased by the criteria. In some schools and departments, discussing the subject criteria could set in train a review of available examinations that makes staff aware of new possibilities. The emphasis within the GCSE upon the freedom of schools to choose their own examinations will, if it is translated into action, give some schools a wider choice than they have had previously. It is quite possible that for many schools the immediate perceived effect of introducing the GCSE will be greater choice rather than less, even though arithmetically the range of choice across England and Wales as a whole has been reduced.

The GCSE involves changes not only in curriculum content but also in the distribution of control over the curriculum. These changes amount to a redistribution of power away from the Examination Boards (and thus the LEAs and universities) towards the government on the one hand, and the schools on the other.

The fundamental feature of this change is indicated in the General Criteria document. In their foreword the Secretaries of State for Education and Science and for Wales welcome the publication of the national criteria as an historic step in which 'the partners in the education service have pooled their wisdom and experience in order to produce nationally agreed statements'. However, later in the same foreword they announce that it is *they* who have approved the texts of the national criteria documents. Unilateral approval and partnership are (of course) incompatible notions. What the Secretaries of State have actually done is to replace negotiation between partners with consultation of inferiors by superiors. The rhetoric of partnership will no doubt remain because it will on occasions be useful to the government, but the underlying reality has clearly changed.

The immediate losers from the change are the Examination Boards. The creation of general criteria requiring approval by the SEC (and thus ultimately by the Secretaries of State) represents a decisive shift in the *de facto* balance of power from Examining Boards to central government, while the development of detailed national criteria covering the majority of subjects largely destroys the independent role of the boards within the education system.

Less obviously, the boards are permanently vulnerable to further government pressure because they are now working to regulations that are ambiguous at a number of points. Interpretation of these regulations is a matter for the SEC, not the boards. Similarly, the approval of particular examination proposals rests with the SEC, and it will be in this approval process that the interpretation of the present criteria will be given concrete form.

This, though, sees the situation only in a static way. But the creation of a permanent review mechanism for the criteria marks a crucial long-term shift in curriculum policy. It is axiomatic that change tends to favour the strong. In the GCSE, we see central government both creating a dominant position for itself, and ensuring that any future changes will be the ones that have its approval. It has done this not by taking over the Examination Boards lock, stock and barrel, but by nationalizing the crucial curriculum policy-making function, leaving to the boards the less interesting role of implementing and administering the examination syllabuses that result.

The grouping of the boards into five Examining Groups is a very important element in the redistribution of control. One effect of this is to reduce the organizations the government has to deal with to a manageable number (although the fact that five is the conventional number of subordinates that one superior should be able to control effectively is no doubt coincidental!). With the introduction of the GCSE the boards had the task of simultaneously reorganizing themselves and reacting to the substantive curriculum proposals in the national criteria. Faced with the problems created by structural changes, it is not surprising that the boards were unable to make as full and as considered a contribution to the policy debate as they might have done.

The other main organizational thrust of the GCSE proposals has been to transfer power from the boards to the individual schools and the departments within them. As we have already seen, the fact that schools are able to choose from the examinations offered by all boards may increase a school's range of choice in practical terms. This tendency will be strengthened in so far as the criteria (and perhaps competition between boards for the schools' custom) make the actual examinations offered more similar than is the case at present. One possible outcome might be that each Examining Group will try to offer a set of examinations in a given subject that covers the range of options allowed by the national criteria, so as to protect their share of the market. In that event, it would become proportionately easier for schools to move from one board to another, because the disruption involved in teaching terms would be somewhat less than is the case at present.

The scale of movement by schools between boards will partly depend upon how the boards (and LEAs) react to the attempt to increase competitive and customer pressures upon them. The final relationship between boards could be anything from cooperation in an unobtrusive cartel to cut-throat competition. Whatever the result, it will determine the real degree of substantive choice schools have between syllabuses.

One feature which will undoubtedly increase the role schools and teachers have in the new system is the growing importance it will give to coursework. Indeed this could prove to be one of the most significant influences upon a department's choice of boards when the content offered is broadly similar. In this respect the popularity of the coursework-only examinations already approved for English will be particularly interesting to see.

In many respects, Conservative governments under Margaret Thatcher have been of a distinctly different kind from their predecessors. They have not been conservative in the sense that they seek to maintain the status quo; on the contrary, they have been a highly innovatory force in many fields, viewing their task as the radical transformation of Britain.

Nor are they conservative in the traditional Tory sense in that they support high culture and an organic 'one nation' conception of society, with its emphasis upon interdependence and shared values. The philosophy of the new Conservatism, in so far as it can be said to have one, can be characterized in terms of efficiency, competition, rationalism, centralism, individual gain and a monetary definition of wealth.

The real danger to such an administration is not the radical Left, indeed, the continued existence of a noisy body of support for simplistic Marxism is probably essential to the survival of radical Conservatism. The threat comes rather from the political centre, and in particular from the traditional Tories who form a part of it. Many of the innovations the government has introduced have been aimed precisely at challenging the assumptions shared by moderates of various hues. One example of this has been the drive to replace consensual working practices by ones based upon conflict channelled by contract and regulation rather than mutual respect and agreement. It is against this background that the government's creation of the SEC (and indeed most of its educational policies) can best be understood.

While the introduction of the GCSE has undoubtedly shifted power in favour of the government it is not clear whether the present arrangements are seen by the government as final or as an essential first step towards an even greater centralization and homogenization of education.

The changes to date do not amount to a full-blown centralization of curriculum control, although they go a long way towards it. The essential change is that a mechanism is now available that allows the government to move, when it so wishes, towards a fully centralized system.

The key to this is that the SEC has been given the task of continuously monitoring the criteria. This will enable it (and consequently the government) to make further changes as the effectiveness or otherwise of the present regulations becomes clear. Less obviously, the new system makes it possible to develop a single centrally coordinated curriculum plan for linking what in a commercial context would be called market research, sales analysis and research and product development.

The Examining Groups who have ready access to examination results, need to meet shared national criteria. The examinations presented by the Groups will have partially overlapping sets of objectives, often with specified mark allocations for particular categories of objectives. Consequently, the results from different boards and syllabuses will for the first time become directly comparable in certain important respects. The government's requirement that the SEC monitor the system implies that detailed information on the results should be made available to the Council. Once procedures to monitor such information on a routine basis are computerized, it becomes possible for the government to carry out as a matter of course a wide variety of annual comparisons between boards, Examining Groups, and categories of students, and to use the results of this to modify both examinations and the role of the boards further. This sort of information would also provide a directly usable source of data for identifying ways in which INSET and initial training objectives should be modified and could be used to establish educational research priorities centrally by picking out specific areas of weakness in the results obtained. The similarity of this to the possibilities created by the work of the APU might be noted.

The creation of the SEC and the GCSE in its present form marks a dramatic change in the way in which central government influences the curriculum. The key feature here is the replacement of *ad hoc* national working parties reporting on specific problems by a centrally directed process of continuous curriculum and examination system review, linking the inputs of government (such as the allocation of research, INSET, and other funds) to the outcome in terms of examination results.

Under the previous system information, problems, funds and innovation proposals could arise from almost any part of the educational community, and innovations could make their way into the schools by a range of alternative routes. The creation of the SEC will centralize much of the influence over innovation as well as over the examinations. In so doing, it will open the way to a realignment of forces within education with implications going far beyond the immediate issues.

One significant indication of the government's intention to move to a fully centralized system would be any attempt to tighten up the links between assessment and objectives in the many subject areas where the national criteria are at present relatively open. Another would be pressure for

Examining Groups to provide the government with examination results in a form that allowed it to carry out comparability studies of the kind described above. These are probably the only essential changes needed to move to a fully centralized system. Although they would impinge upon the schools very little when first introduced, their longer term implications for schools would be considerable.

Characteristic of the present government are attempts to increase its influence by thinning out intermediate centres of power between itself and individual groups or organizations. In the short term this may not appear to affect things greatly at grass roots level, but once the intermediate centres are weakened it is far harder for individuals or local groups to make their views count. This will be so in the case of the GCSE. Under the old system the task facing an innovative school would have been to persuade a local board of the need for change (with the option in some cases of trying another board if they got no support). The creation of national criteria means that a school or group of schools wishing to innovate in ways incompatible with the criteria has an almost insuperable problem. This reduces the power of a school to get the sort of assessment strategy that it wants, if only by raising the cost of innovation in terms of effort to a point where most schools cannot or will not pay it.

A fully centralized system also increases the pressure upon individual boards and schools to conform to the majority view. Where the policies of a school or board are not easily compared with those of others, there is no such pressure. But once an organization is identified as having a different policy to the majority it is vulnerable to challenges. Logically this is (of course) nonsense. There is no reason to think that on issues of curriculum balance, or choice of objectives, the majority view is any more likely to be right than that of a thoughtful and serious-minded minority. But psychologically, it is the case that majority opinions are less likely to be challenged. Given the implicit (and equally indefensible) assumption in the whole GCSE exercise that precise criteria and assessment weightings can be rationally decided centrally, it is natural that parents and others will assume that schools and boards resisting majority opinion are in some way failing to provide a proper education for their students.

A further danger in increased government involvement in curriculum and assessment is that it sucks examinations into the general arena of political and occupational conflicts between the government and teachers. As the major source of teachers' salaries the government is bound, given its other policies, to be in opposition to teachers as employees. But it is vital to the effective working of schools that salary and employment issues are, as far as possible, kept separate from discussions about what to teach and how to assess it. The teachers' dispute, that started in 1985, overlapped with the introduction of the GCSE, making this separation hard to maintain in the short term. My point though is that the nature and remit of the SEC is such that it could easily become a permanent forum for conflicts between teachers and government, given that the role of the boards as impartial intermediaries will now be much reduced.

What then of the alternatives to greater government power? Here there are two separate issues. One is the extent to which further centralization is desirable, and the other is the appropriate role of the government within whatever degree of centralization there is to be. This distinction in turn sows the seeds of disunity amongst those opposing governmentally dominated central control. Some oppose both centralism and greater governmental influence, while others may be prepared to accept greater central direction so long as their own views are likely to be influential in setting that direction.

Those opposed to centralism of any kind will no doubt be pressing for as flexible an interpretation of the criteria as possible, for an increased emphasis upon coursework, and for the active development of Mode 3 assessment. But it is hard to see how this ground can be held at the local level unless there is also strong support for it at the centre. In this respect, the decentralists will paradoxically have to accept a degree of centralization in their own organization if they are to be successful.

If an alternative to growing government power were to emerge, an early sign would be the creation of a network of horizontal contacts between those groups whose autonomy has been reduced by the new structure. These would include the boards, LEAs, the teacher organizations, specialist subject associations and the providers of teacher education. A second sign of resistance might be an insistence that whatever statistical information on GCSE entries and results was available to the government would automatically be in the public domain, allowing all interested parties to share in its interpretation. Modern computers and communications systems would make this entirely practicable. Third, there might be moves to establish regular contacts with outside parties such as employers, managers, unions and parents. Direct access to their views might be more valuable rather than automatically accepting the government's interpretation of, for instance, the needs of industry.

Paradoxically the reorganization of the boards may itself provide the basis for a return to something closer to a relationship of equality between central government and the other groups involved. In drawing the Examination Boards into five groups, the government has also created the framework for organized resistance to its further increase in power. No doubt the activities of these groups can all be centrally monitored in a way that the work of individual boards never could. But the new structure also allows the boards to coordinate their responses and formulate joint initiatives, perhaps through the central coordinating body that has been created for the Examining Groups. While the role of this body might turn out to be purely technical, it could be used more purposefully by the boards to generate and implement policies of their own.

But will the boards and Examining Groups accept the competitive role allocated to them in the GCSE structure? Protective cooperation is at least as likely a response. As the future extension of the government's influence will partly depend upon creating and maintaining an atmosphere of rivalry between the boards, this is a crucial issue.

The subject associations too may gain influence in the new structure. In the creation of the various national criteria members of these associations often had an important role, and the existence of the criteria now provides an explicit framework within which both theoretical and practical curriculum debates can (and indeed must) be carried on. This is likely to increase the importance of the associations as national foci for organizing initiatives coming from specialist teachers. The teacher unions too will have opportunities to regain at least some of their influence, provided that they can coordinate their responses with those of the boards and specialist associations.

Finally there might be moves to revise the SEC itself. It is already clear that the SEC is not simply a transparent medium through which the government's wishes will be transmitted. It is already developing its own ideas and emphases, and as an organization charged with working both with the government and with the other ex-partners, it will have to be responsive to both. However, the fact that the Council's members are government appointees makes it inevitable that the influence of the government will be predominant.

One obvious possibility is that there will be attempts to remove the SEC from narrowly political influence by reforming the method of appointing its members. One approach might be to press for all members to be acceptable to all the major political parties. This would give a considerable degree of stability to the Council in policy terms, but would be likely to exclude radical minority opinion from both the left and right. A fairer scheme might be to give each political party the right to make a number of nominations, and to leave the Council with the right to coopt additional members. The effect of this would be to transform the Council from a government body to a broadly representative one, able to act as an effective broker between the various parties. This would also ensure enough continuity in policy to allow for long-term developments. Given the time-scale needed for effective innovation in schools, this is essential.

Whether we are going to see either more or less centralized control in the future is impossible to say. One ironic possibility is that the Conservatives will complete their nationalization of the examination system just in time to allow their Socialist successors to make the most of the situation. Perhaps more likely is that the next administration will, whatever its party political complexion, be closer to the centre ground than those of Margaret Thatcher's have been. If so, it will be fascinating to see whether the current rhetoric from moderates about decentralization and devolution of power survives once the power is theirs to use.

SECTION II

CRITERIA AND TECHNIQUES

Chapter 5
COURSEWORK
Tim Horton (*Open University*)

The use of coursework in assessment implies one of the less radical changes in curriculum practice with the introduction of GCSE. Most secondary schools have routinely used continuous assessments in their work leading to both GCE and CSE. The expansion of internal assessment with the arrival of CSE in the 1960s was remarkable, and allowed the Schools Council in 1975 to conduct a very thorough review of a variety of practices that have largely remained in place for a decade (Hoste and Bloomfield, 1975).

Initially, coursework assessment was a common feature of Mode 3 examining, used by teachers providing alternatives for those dissatisfied with Mode 1. Hoste and Bloomfield quote teachers using continuous assessment:

> We had already done a Mode 1 with these particular pupils and we found that we required a syllabus more suitable to their needs. We did it to give them a broader syllabus than that already available. (Hoste and Bloomfield, 1975, p. 50)

> Year after year we have candidates who go in for the examination and we know they are worth grade 1 but they come out with grade 4 or sometimes grade 5. This is very frustrating for them and for us. (Hoste and Bloomfield, 1975, p. 50)

There were early concerns about the validity of assessment using terminal examinations, but the process of developing Mode 3 continuously assessed courses stimulated curriculum development and change in a number of ways. First, it allowed teachers to provide what they regarded as more relevant and appropriate divisions in the timetable. Community studies examinations, for example, began in this way. Second, teachers needed to attend closely to the interaction between syllabus design and judgements on the performances of students. Third, continuous assessment in Mode 3 marked a more collegial approach to discussion on subjects, their aims and objectives, and teaching methods. Not only were Mode 3 syllabuses often presented by local consortia of schools, but the moderating process itself encouraged reviews. The task of deciding grade levels might technically concentrate on distinctions between, say, grades 1 and 2 but the wider educational implications were quickly recognized in these debates.

Mode 3 and continuous assessment ceased to be the preserve of the dissenting teacher, becoming instead the powerhouse for some highly original, even unpredictable, initiatives in the secondary curriculum. These new emphases on assessments during the course were able simultaneously to deal both with the psychological problems of stress and anxiety so often associated with terminal assessment, and to extend the curriculum by emphasizing skills rather than recall. Yet while teachers were increasingly conscious of connections between the syllabus and its assessment scheme, the establishment of the former usually preceded the creation of the latter.

GCSE, through the operation of the criteria framework, reverses the position. The onus is now on the teacher to justify the greater validity and reliability of coursework assessments against terminal assessment. In addition the SEC argues that the main aim of coursework assessment is to make 'what is important measurable, rather than of making what is measurable important' (SEC, 1985).

These concerns for validity might operate to limit the scope of coursework assessment. Yet the SEC in *Working Paper 2: Coursework Assessment in GCSE* (SEC, 1985) in fact provides a long list of possible benefits for its use in the new system. These fall into four broad categories:

1 *Psychological:* a release from anxiety engendered by a one-off assessment at the end of the course and stress, resulting in fatal errors such as misreading questions; greater reinforcement on task performance; and inculcating a sense of discovery.
2 *Technical:* an increase in reliability through a fuller representation of abilities; an extension in the range of student abilities manageable in the teaching of a syllabus.
3 *Pedagogic:* a vehicle for cross-curricular assessment; closer attention to the application of knowledge and skills to the outside world.
4 *Curricular:* greater attention to criteria for subject and details of syllabus; a shift towards planning for students' experiences.

The encouragement of coursework is considerable. The main dilemmas of this form of assessment are inherent in the implications for schools and college of its introduction to nearly all syllabuses in all institutions, and the implications for school-based curricular development.

Hitherto, many teachers have not been required to use coursework assessment. Indeed, selected schools, particularly, have avoided any involvement with these practices altogether. The extent of the expansion of recording and reviewing implied now for all teachers in schools is formidable and likely to be keenly felt as the second cohort of GCSE candidates enters the new system. Coursework encourages students to use and develop techniques for making and recording accurate detail of a subject, and the same requirement now falls upon teachers.

The debate about the administrative consequences of these procedures has been remarkably limited. Yet the problems of storing, processing, retrieving and analysing coursework marks could impose an enormous organizational burden upon schools. The paucity of administrative support staff, particularly at departmental and faculty level in secondary schools, will be increasingly exposed. The need to develop systems to cope with the increasing scale of coursework marks may force the rapid development of computer software capable of offsetting this load. In the *Geography* guide (Orrell and Tolley, 1986), some existing facilities are described, but the need for sophistication necessary for the task might be compared to the requirement for increasingly better programmes for timetabling in schools.

The other major decision, falling again to teachers in their design of Mode 3 syllabuses or their choice of Mode 1 syllabus, concerns the decisions about when exactly, and how regularly, to assess. The major difficulty is that a significant percentage of a final grade could be awarded at an early stage, misrepresenting ability at the termination of the course. In the case of several of the major subjects, English is an example, syllabuses have been accepted by the SEC which includes 100 per cent internal assessment. The validity or, in public terms, equity of these assessment practices on a widespread scale may come under increasing attention.

Coursework does not, for the majority of teachers, raise any fundamentally new issues. As a feature of the new system it is the sheer volume of new administrative demands that is likely to become most critical. While a minority of schools, particularly in the private sector, will find more that is new, it is linkage to the moderating procedures that now offers, for the first time to all teachers, ways of using examining networks for structuring new curriculum patterns – an issue discussed by Harry Torrance in Chapter 14 of this book.

REFERENCES

Hoste, R. and Bloomfield, B. (1975) *Continuous Assessment in the CSE: Opinion and Practice*, Schools Council Examinations Bulletin 31, Evans/Methuen, London

Orrell, K. and Tolley, H. (1986) *Geography (GCSE: A Guide for Teachers)*, Open University Press, Milton Keynes

Secondary Examinations Council (1985) *Coursework Assessment in GCSE*. Working Paper 2, SEC, London

CHAPTER 6
ACCENTUATING THE POSITIVE
Tim Horton (*Open University*)

In the otherwise dry General Criteria, there is the commitment towards an examination system that demonstrates what students 'know, understand and can do' (SEC, 1985). This phrase has provided the new system with a popular slogan. Amid the recent stormy politics of education where a degree of unison has been rare, it provides echoes of a time when consensus ruled more widely. Even if ministerial hopes of raising the standards of achievement fail to materialize, this commitment to positive assessment will, in retrospect, be seen as something of a landmark.

There is official caution, however. While extolling the virtues of positive assessment, the Secondary Examinations Council tends not to make too many lavish claims about the success of its implementation – at least in the short term. What, then, are the issues, and why is time needed?

Positive assessment has given rise to differentiated assessment. To quote part of paragraph 16 of the General Criteria:

> All examinations must be designed in such a way as to ensure proper consultation so that candidates across the ability range are given opportunities to demonstrate what they know, understand and can do. Differentiated papers, or differentiated questions within papers, will be required accordingly in all subjects [. . .]. (SEC, 1985)

The political significance of this was that it took the 16+ out of an impasse it had entered in the 1970s. The hesitation of the Callaghan administration (with Mrs Shirley Williams as Secretary of State) over the Schools Council's recommendations revealed splits not only between the political parties but also within them. Yet, as the series of reviews of 16+ (including the 1978 Waddell Report) were made public, the idea of a common system gained agreement. The issues then became, what is *technically* feasible?, and what does this mean for *teaching and the organization of schools*?.

I shall look at the issue of differentiation using three foci – the political, the technical and the pedagogic.

Reform in education since the war has frequently been achieved not by a meeting of minds, or even compromise, but by the establishment of new systems and practices that allow all interests to claim success for their distinct advocacies. In effect the shareholders of the education system (local authorities, teachers' unions, government departments, etc.) make a selective rationale in support of change. For example, the introduction of CSE in the 1960s was variously deemed worthwhile because it (1) extended certification to a new group of students; (2) allowed finer discrimination between students; (3) permitted national oversight of the curriculum; (4) gave power to teachers to develop new forms of curricula and assessment practice. However, the 16+ proposals coming from educational bodies including, most importantly, the Schools Council, did not initially allow for a similar concordat. How working compromises were finally achieved is examined by Brian Salter and Ted Tapper, and by Peter Scrimshaw, in this book, but it is worth giving emphasis to the issue of how a struggle over teacher control was deflected into a technical argument concerning assessment using criterion reference approaches.

Teacher control over the curriculum was most fully enshrined in the objectives of the Schools Council. In 1964, the Council had adopted the Lockwood Committee's report recommendation that 'each school should have the fullest possible measure of responsibility for its own work, with its own curriculum and teaching methods [. . .]'. The significance of this objective, at the time and subsequently, was threefold. First it was an effective rejoinder to the then Ministry of Education's attempt to enter the 'secret garden of the curriculum'. Second, it posed a dilemma for a young organization seeking to establish representative democracy. Who best represents schools on a national body? The failure of various attempts to create a General Teaching Council meant these rights were passed to teacher unions and, to a lesser extent, local authorities. (Arguably, from the outset, there was a tension that the Council could not itself satisfactorily resolve, particularly after the Association of Education Committees was wound up in the mid-1970s.) Third, the objective also enshrined the principle that the creation of new curriculum should lead to appropriate assessment. This primacy of curricular over assessment concerns was reflected in the organizational structure of the Council itself – a matter later noted by Nancy Trenaman in her report on the Council:

> In spite of the Council's own emphasis on the necessity for curriculum and examinations to be considered by the same body, any link between the Examinations Committee and the Professional Committee, where the

main work on the curriculum was drawn together, was in practice tenuous. (DES, 1981a, p. 22)

Until the 'great debate' got under way, education reformers were united in taking the view that assessment-led change could only stultify useful curriculum innovation. While none doubted the continuing influence of examinations on teaching, those united in favour of change looked forward to different new horizons. Some envisaged teaching culminating in teacher-devised papers on school-designed syllabuses – a rapid development of Mode 3. Others anticipated an extension of continuous assessment, using personal records of achievement.

During the 'great debate' (which coincided with the review of the Schools Council's 16+ proposals) there were not many voices to be heard dissenting markedly from the reformers' aspirations. Critics however did raise awkward issues about the capacity of a teacher-monitored system to achieve other ends too. Thus, a new focus was on the sizeable minority of school leavers who, despite comprehensivization, achieved no passes at either GCE or CSE. Next, attention was given to the width of the curriculum for many pupils after the early years of secondary schooling. Was there a need to provide again a core of necessary subjects for all pupils? The evidence that large numbers of students were not studying a core was never strong, but a few instances were enough to raise alarm. Therefore, in spite of other evidence that examinations were being taken by nine out of ten students, both GCE and CSE were seen as inadequate in their reach and distorting in their effect. Reformers advocating the importance of students' interests stood doubly accused of ignoring a minority, and of failing a majority.

What emerged as the debate continued was not only greater stridency from the new conservatives, but also a shift in the advocacy of the 'old guard' reformers. The vision of the withering away of examinations was replaced by a full embrace of examination-led reform. Examinations would now be the vehicle for all, regardless of ability, to have access to a common culture. Learner-centredness, the predominant leaning since the 1960s, gave way to a liberal humanism in which needs could again be socially, and politically, determined. With fortune, the new contracts to be forged between teachers and the taught could retain authority with the profession, and even reinvigorate it. The new humanistic stance was given a text through the publication of *A View of the Curriculum* (DES, 1980) by Her Majesty's Inspectorate that, with some modification only, reintroduced the modes of experience in Paul Hirst's work.

In this new position, the reconstructed reformers were better able to find common ground with the new conservatives who were interested in both subjects and in standards, each being relevant to improving the national economic performance. In curricular terms, dissonance was avoided through agreement on student entitlements, expressed not simply in terms of subjects to be taken, but processes to be experienced. Tentative agreement could be founded in *The School Curriculum* (DES, 1981b) and given further treatment in a succession of HMI reports and eventually in the subject criteria of GCSE. In examination terms, the new agreement would require a commitment towards the assessment of all on more common bases. This went further than the coexistence, or merger of GCE and CSE, and would raise technical issues of great importance.

I implied, earlier, that under the aegis of the Schools Council, examination reform took on a secondary role to curricular reform. This was partly due to the fear of examination board authority, but also to the failure of the Council's reform proposals (especially 'N' and 'F' examinations). None the less, the technical work of the Council, conducted with the support and advice of the National Foundation for Educational Research, and the boards themselves, was considerable. Yet while the reports issued were numerous, they were based on work that assumed a passive rather than active role for assessment in schools; and also for a system that embraced a target group of only three-fifths of the ability range. A considerable proportion of the work concerned comparability – between systems (GCE and CSE), between boards, and between subjects. In short, the technical team had provided ample evidence about normative assessment that would be of somewhat limited value in the new circumstances where criterion-referencing was needed. In order to denote rises and falls in the standards of pupils, relatively fixed descriptions of grades would be needed, rather than expression of students relative performance. In the Schools Council Examination Bulletin 32 (Deale, 1975) the technical tasks inherent in this were seen as daunting. Further, the educational impact concerned the author:

[. . .] it can be misleading to both pupil and parents if they are told that the child has worked very well, to the best of his ability, all through the school, only to find at the end of the course that he has attained no more than a very modest level indeed. (Deale, 1975)

None the less, the new consensus on examining required differentiated assessment and not simply examinations that discriminated. The purpose of differentiated assessment is to show what students know, understand, and can do, rather than suggest the extent of their inability. The needs of a differentiated system immediately require a reasonable degree of common agreement about the range of knowledge, understanding, and action encompassed within a subject – hence the establishment of criteria. But more testing still would be the evolution of techniques that would provide assessments which did not abrogate the principle of common access. The Secondary Examination Council, inheriting the coordinating task from the Schools Council, was in large measure bound by the technical experience and research findings of an earlier time. It favoured a range of strategies that borrowed from comparability experiments in stepped questions and papers, and differentiated papers (for which a specific range of grades are reserved).

It coupled this with the controversial concept of neutral stimulus – a task neutral with respect to difficulty. The new Council did not disguise the difficulty posed by differentiated assessment. Indeed, its *Working Paper 1: Differentiated Assessment in GCSE* (SEC, 1985) is a remarkably honest statement of the problems to be anticipated in any chosen scheme. In essence the difficulties revolve around three issues:
1   the language used to explain a task (particularly important for neutral stimulus);
2   the engagement of students (are the tasks always encouraging the student to express the range of his or her ability?);
3   the attack on assessment (should students be channelled in their sequencing of tasks?)

The political shift of education for all, now implying also examining for all, at least in a medium term future, caught teachers and examination boards by surprise. With alacrity they amended well-known psychometric techniques suited to efficient normative assessment, to the new requirements. Several innovations, including the use of grade criteria, were borrowed also from the testing of mastery, having separate origins in diagnostic work. The major problem, however, was that if knowledge of differentiated assessment was scant as far as terminal assessment was concerned, it was virtually non-existent for continuous assessment. It is interesting that the techniques addressed in the Secondary Examination Council paper and the Open University/SEC guides, issued in 1986, were largely taken up with the preparation of papers; less attention is given to differentiated coursework assessment. It is either argued that this only involves the logical extension of principles to the setting of class assignments, or that it is less important as, in practice, differentiation is a less foreign concept in the day-to-day activity of schools. Both arguments are contestable. If differentiated terminal examining can be demonstrated, it is as an assessment given in a short period of time – and it is far from easy to see the extension of this to, say, two years of student study. Would students be able to go back on work offered for assessment? Second, teachers, I suggest, may well assign separate tasks to students, but usually on a basis of discrimination rather than differentiation.

Differentiation implies, logically, a high degree of individual task-setting, a mode of operating that is exacting and heavily demanding upon material and professional resources. The individualization of syllabuses is perhaps attractive and echoes the spirit of learner-centredness. Yet at the same time it exists in tension with syllabus designs and subject criteria that are moving towards conformity.

The evolution of the political debate on the secondary curriculum, and the ill-preparedness of examining bodies to deal with the new assumptions on a technical level, has forced upon schools the burden of deciding new curricular and organizational arrangements. Differentiation provides an employer with a surer guide to the quality of its new recruits through positive assessment – a considerable benefit in a buyer's market. Yet teachers are left to determine solutions that give individuals expression under a collective system. Time will show whether the professional acumen of teachers can overcome the current technical shortcomings using differentiated assessment, or whether the GCSE will require a new political initiative to make the system comprehensible and practical.

REFERENCES

Deale, R.N. (1975) *Assessment and Testing in the Secondary School*, Schools Council Examination Bulletin 32, Evans/Methuen Educational, London
DES (1980) *A View of the Curriculum*, HMI Series: Matters for Discussion 1.1, HMSO, London
DES (1981a) *Review of the Schools Council* (the Trenaman Report), HMSO, London
DES (1981b) *The School Curriculum*, HMSO, London
Secondary Examination Council (1985) *Differentiated Assessment in GCSE*, Working Paper 1, SEC, London
Waddell Report (1978)

Chapter 7
ENGLISH
Maggie MacLure (*University of East Anglia*)

> The first question that has to be asked about any system of assessment [. . .] is whether it has a benign effect on the curriculum. (National Association for the Teaching of English, 1980, p. 2)

Although it will be some years before we can answer the question raised in the quotation at the opening of this chapter, the GCSE criteria for English seem to support at least in principle, many of the promising developments in the teaching of English, and its assessment, that have taken place since. The English teaching community therefore hopes that the effects of the GCSE system will indeed be 'benign'.

ENGLISH AS COMMUNICATION

One of the most important aspects of the GCSE criteria is the overall emphasis on English as *meaningful communication*. This is clearly stated in its first aim: 'The course should seek to develop the ability of students to [. . .] communicate accurately, appropriately and effectively in speech and writing' (National Criteria for English, para. 1.1.1). The emphasis, therefore, is upon students' ability to use their language resources effectively for a wide range of genuinely communicative purposes.

One outcome of this is the acknowledgement that spoken, as well as written language, is an essential aspect of competence in English. Indeed the equal billing given to talk and writing in the English criteria – with compulsory assessment of oral communication for all candidates – is one of the major innovations of the GCSE system; it is, also, one of its more controversial aspects as will be seen.

One of the basic principles of this view of English is that writing and talking are done for particular purposes, with particular audiences, or listeners, in mind. Indeed, it is these very factors that guide writers or speakers to decide which style to adopt, which topics to highlight, and so on. And, since we need both to write and to speak for many different purposes and audiences, competence in language involves the ability to *vary* our language resources to meet a wide range of demands. One of the problems with many of the CSE and O-level English syllabuses has been that they have encouraged an extremely narrow range of writing skills, largely focusing on the discursive essay – a form of writing whose purpose and intended audience are often obscure to the struggling writer. The GCSE English criteria recognize the diversity inherent in language use, stating that syllabuses must encourage students to 'show a sense of audience and an awareness of style in both formal and informal situations', and provide for 'a range of experiences' in talk, reading, and writing (*National Criteria for English*, Section A, paras. 2.1.6 and 3). In one syllabus, for instance, the range of writing to be covered includes:

(a) personal response to such stimuli as pictures, music, poetry and prose;

(b) description of, and reflection upon personal experience in narrative, anecdote or autobiography;

(c) fictional or imaginative accounts and description;

(d) writing which conveys an attitude, or aims to evoke a mood;

(e) objective description or explanation of processes from knowledge and experience;

(f) accounts or explanations of how problems might be solved, or tasks performed;

(g) discussion of issues, exploration and evaluation of arguments, presentation of opinions or conclusions, persuasion from differing points of view;

(h) communicating sensitive and informed personal response to a wide variety of reading. (London and East Anglian Group, GCSE syllabus in English)

Potentially, therefore, students have the chance to develop a much wider range of language resources than in the past. To take the example of demonstrating response to reading materials: instead of being asked to 'give an account of' an incident from a book, or to 'state how far you agree with' some view expressed; students might be asked to write a newspaper account of an incident, retell the incident from the point of view of a minor character, rework the incident for younger readers, or write a poem prompted by the incident. They might write a review article, or design a book-jacket, or construct the script of a radio interview with the characters. They might even paint a picture or draw a cartoon depicting certain events, make a video

documentary on an issue raised in the book, or mount a dramatic reconstruction.

Each of these activities requires both linguistic, and interpretive skills of quite different kinds – the ones I have mentioned represent only a few of the ideas which English teachers have been developing in recent years both, to make written texts accessible to students across the ability range, and to broaden their language experiences in meaningful and rewarding ways (for example, Scott, 1983).

It remains to be seen, how able the examining groups are at actively encouraging work of this kind. Will they accept, for example some of the more innovative possibilities, such as art work or video tapes for the purposes of assessment. Although the *National Criteria for English* state, for example, that all of the objectives for English 'are capable of being tested in both speech and writing' (Section A, para. 2), current syllabuses seem to recognize only written submissions, in both their examination papers, and in their coursework regulations. Spoken coursework assessment, for instance, is a possibility which has not yet been pursued in the syllabuses.

Reading for meaning and personal enjoyment

The emphasis on communication in the English criteria applies not only to the transmission skills of writing and speaking, it also applies to reading and – though this is less clearly stated – listening. These modes of language have, often and mistakenly, been considered to be in the main, passive activities. The ubiquitous reading comprehension, for instance, often asked students to accomplish little more than literal paraphrasing of words and phrases, or summaries of content (Barnes and Seed, 1981). The GCSE criteria, however, encourage active reading in such a way that students are encouraged to interpret, evaluate, and understand how writers achieve their effects; and to relate what they have read to their own, and to others', experiences. So as to be able to do this effectively, they are given whole tests to read rather than mere extracts alone (*National Criteria for English*, Section A, para. 3). The criteria also recognize that, particularly in the reading of literature, students' own personal response to what they have read is valuable and must be acknowledged (Section B, para. 1.1.1).

Using language skills in combination

As well as stressing the importance of all four of the modes of language, namely, reading, writing, listening and speaking, the English criteria recognize that the interrelatedness of these modes in communication in real life:

'The use of language represents a variety of linguistic skills and modes of language. It is not intended that these should be assessed in isolation' (Section A, para. 4.1). Similarly, referring particularly to oral communication, the criteria note that 'emphasis should be placed on the interrelatedness of speaking and listening' (Section A, para. 3.1). Ideally, therefore, syllabuses should encourage activities which involve the use of two or more modes in conjunction. This could involve a sequence of related activities: for instance, conducting tape-recorded interviews to gather information on a theme or issue, making notes from the tapes, pooling the information gathered in group discussion, reading background sources to support the findings of the group, reporting back to a large audience, planning a campaign arising out of the group's work, and so on. The compulsory coursework component of GCSE syllabuses provides scope for activities of this kind, allowing students to coordinate their oral, writing, and reading resources. In current papers set by the Examining Groups, however, the traditional – and in many ways artificial – separation of the language modes looks likely to continue. The English syllabus of the London and East Anglian Group, for instance, preserves the traditional distinction between expression and understanding and response, which are to be assessed in two separate papers with these titles. And the requirement of the criteria that oral communication must be separately assessed works against the integration of spoken and written language.

ENGLISH LITERATURE

Although the National Criteria state that English is to be regarded as 'a single unified course', the historical divide between language and literature is maintained when it comes to assessment, since the GCSE English courses lead to separate assessments: one in English, and the other, as an additional choice, in English literature. My comments so far have been directed mainly to the criteria as these relate to English, or to those aspects which apply equally to both subject areas. Certain aspects of the criteria relating particularly to English literature should also be mentioned.

The GCSE criteria envisage an approach to the study of literary texts which goes beyond 'mere recall' (*National Criteria for English*, Section B, para. 4.3), encouraging students both to express a personal response and to recognize and appreciate the ways in which writers use language and achieve their effects (Section B, para. 1). In order to minimize a reliance on memory, syllabuses can allow access to texts, both in coursework and in the form of plain texts in the written examinations.

One of the most notable aspects of the criteria for English literature is the provision for a wider *range* of texts than was generally available in the traditional *set texts* for O-level and CSE syllabus. Students following GCSE syllabuses are expected to undertake both detailed study and wider reading, they may, consequently, be offered a wide personal choice in selecting texts (*National Criteria for English*, Section B, paras. 2.1 and 2.2). It is encouraging too, that, according to the criteria, one of the ways in which Examining Groups may promote this breadth of reading is to 'attend to the scope of what is traditionally regarded as the canon of English literature in recognition that awareness of the richness of cultural diversity is one of the rewards of the study of literature' (Section B, para. 2). The English criteria reiterate here one of the important requirements of the General Criteria (para. 19) for all subjects, that is, the need to avoid bias of various kinds. I would hope, for instance, that the under-representation on English literature syllabuses in the past, of works by women novelists, dramatists and poets, and particularly contemporary women writers, will ultimately be remedied; and that Examining Groups and teachers will take account of the extent to which the range of books offered for study addresses the interests of both girls and boys.

ORAL COMMUNICATION

One of the most controversial aspects of the new criteria for English is the requirement of a compulsory assessment of oral communication. We have already seen that the criteria recognize the importance of talk as an essential element of competence in English – most English teachers would agree that the ability to communicate successfully in speech is vitally important, particularly since we devote much more time, throughout our lives, to talk rather than to writing. However, although most teachers would agree that oral work deserves more attention than it has been given in schools in the past, opinion is divided as to whether or not it is a progressive step to insist on its formal *assessment.*

Those who advocate oral assessment often do so on the grounds that its appearance on examination syllabuses is likely to promote the development of oral work in the classroom. Certainly, there is some force to this argument. Teachers have often cited the time constraints of covering the content of the old syllabuses – their exclusive focus (at O-level) being on the written word – as one of the main obstacles to the introduction of more spoken language work. It can be argued, too, that students deserve credit for their oral abilities, which may be considerably in advance of their writing skills: and that employers will be encouraged to value more highly these valuable qualities if they are formally accredited.

On the other hand, there are those who oppose oral assessment, either because of the perceived difficulties of assessing it reliably, or because they fear that assessment may actually do more harm than good to the cause of promoting good practice in oral work in the classroom. Taking the latter, and more important point first, there are fears that the assessment of talk in the GCSE may simply perpetuate on a wider scale the sterile exercises characteristic of many Mode 1 CSE orals. These typically included reading aloud, giving a prepared 'lecturette' – often on a prescribed topic – or holding an uncomfortable interview about one's hobbies to one or more assessors. It would be difficult to defend such a narrow range of artificial tasks, carried out in inauspicious and often stressful situations, as positive models of the richness and diversity of spoken communication. The GCSE English criteria appear to recognize the limitations of this view of oral assessment, requiring syllabuses to provide for a range of experiences of oral communication (Section A, para. 3), and stating that 'the interactive nature of listening and speaking cannot be demonstrated solely by reading aloud or delivering a talk' (Section A, para. 5.2). However, the criteria, otherwise, are disappointingly vague about the kinds of speaking and listening activities which should be encouraged, making specific mention only of interviews and group discussion 'with some aim or goal' as instances of situations within which oral skills can be assessed.

However, there are those who feel that any attempt to assess oral communication can only have negative effects. One commentator on the GCSE English criteria has argued in the educational press that 'any attempt to impose standardized assessment procedures upon the spoken language is pretty well doomed to distort what we most seek to foster and respect' (Knight, 1985). In the view of this commentator, the imposition of aims or goals upon conversation, and indeed the attempt to assess these in any form, is contrary to the 'spirit of the English language' and cannot take full account of the subtleties of discussion, in which 'silences, half-finished remarks, scarcely verbal promptings and withdrawals may play their part quite as effectively as fully articulated sentences'.

The ways in which oral assessment is approached certainly need careful consideration. It is essential, for instance, to avoid imposing artificial notions of 'good English' on students' language, or conveying attitudes which suggest that the language of speakers of 'non-standard' forms is in any way inferior to that associated with white middle-class speech. It has to be remembered, too, that students may come from communities which observe conventions for communicating that are at variance with those of other speakers. Girls from families of Asian origin, for instance, may find talking in large mixed groups intimidating, since this may conflict with cultural expectations of modesty and reticence.

The issues raised by the compulsory assessment of oral communication are further compounded by the requirement that oral communication must be recorded separately from the grade in English on the examination certificate. This has led to fears that English as a subject will continue to be thought of as fundamentally a matter of reading and writing, with talk being treated as an extra. It does appear that, although the English criteria elsewhere recognize that whilst speaking and listening are as important as the other language modes, there has been a failure of nerve over the formal recognition of this on the examination certificate.

Whilst at this stage, it is difficult to predict what long-term implications oral assessment will have for the English curriculum, my own view is, that the potential is there for redressing the historical imbalance between talk and writing, for promoting new forms of collaborative learning, and for encouraging students to become both versatile and confident speakers. Whether these outcomes are realized, however, will depend on many factors; for instance, it seems unlikely that any real reappraisal of the importance of spoken language in the classroom will take place when syllabuses insist on a single end-of-course assessment rather than the continuous assessment of students' oral work throughout the course. Apart from merely relegating talk to the status of a one-off event, end-of-course tests cannot adequately cover a range of situations, purposes and audiences. They are also likely to penalize those students who find the formality of such occasions stressful – for, they are inevitably more artificial in their demands upon students than assessments of work arising naturally throughout the course. Continuous assessment of oral work, on the other hand, keeps talk on the agenda as a regular part of classroom work, and allows students to demonstrate a range of competences in somewhat more relaxed circumstances – it is, also, more likely to reflect their abilities more accurately since the variations in students' efforts on differing occasions can be balanced, and their strengths and weaknesses on the particular kinds of tasks demanded, can be identified. And since the teacher's evaluations of his or her students' abilities will be based on knowledge of their performance on many different occasions, there will be less danger, particularly in group situations, of penalizing the student who happens, on a single occasion, to feel unable or disinclined to contribute much; or, of overlooking the student whose contributions, though less frequent than those of the other members, may be consistently relevant and thoughtful.

It is vital, however, that teachers should gain experience of developing and evaluating oral work in the classroom. The provisions which the Examining Groups have made for agreement-trials will obviously be of importance here, both in providing opportunities for teachers to get together to discuss examples of pupils' oral work, and the procedures for evaluating them. However, it has to be remembered that the Examining Groups are just as inexperienced as anyone else in oral assessment of the kind I have envisaged here, although some of their members have had experience of CSE oral assessment. There is a need, therefore, for adequate in-service provision in this area, so that teachers may share experiences of organizing their teaching, and their time, in ways which allow them to carry out assessment without interfering with their primary role as teachers.

COURSEWORK IN ENGLISH

Internally assessed coursework must account for at least 20 per cent of all the marks awarded in both English and English literature syllabuses. However, Examining Groups are offering options in English which allow for assessment entirely by coursework. The provision for coursework assessment is one of the most welcome features of the GCSE criteria, since it allows teachers a considerable degree of freedom to develop their own strategies for meeting the objectives of syllabuses, and also overcomes many of the disadvantages of timed written papers as a way of allowing students to demonstrate their abilities in the subject.

The advantages of coursework are many. Opportunities to write and speak for a wide range of purposes, for example, can easily be accomplished in more realistic situations over the duration of a course, than would be possible in the examination room. Students can be asked to write for, and receive feedback from differing audiences in activities such as writing stories for younger children, or letters to their local press, radio station or MP. Similarly, coursework allows students to try out their oral skills in encounters with people other than their classmates and teachers, by, perhaps, interviewing people in their workplace, or by researching in the community. However, as I have already noted, the evidence of such oral activities needs to be presented in some kind of written form so as to qualify as coursework assignments for assessment.

The requirements in the English criteria of sustained reading and writing can be met more easily in coursework. Out-of school visits to films and theatre performances can provide a stimulus for both written and oral work.

The conditions under which students write are also radically altered in coursework: freed from the constraints of writing fair copies at their first attempt, they have time to reflect, to digest ideas and to edit their work in successive drafts. Sequenced tasks involving, planning, background research, collation of information, and presentation of materials can also be undertaken.

Students as well as teachers are likely to benefit from the degree of autonomy in both teaching and learning that coursework offers. Ideally, students will have the chance to follow chosen lines of study, following up issues and themes which are of particular interest to them under the guidance of their teacher.

Teachers vary a great deal in the amount of experience they have of coursework assessment. Some will have entered candidates for coursework-based O-level and CSE examinations for many years, others encountering coursework assessment for the first time, however, face new challenges. This is another area, therefore, in which in-service support would be a valuable supplement to the guidance given by the Examining Groups.

DIFFERENTIATION

Finally, brief mention should be made of the methods of achieving differentiation in English and English literature. Although the subject criteria allow, in principle, for a range of methods, in practice, the Examining Groups have not chosen differentiated papers, or sections within papers, for candidates of different perceived levels of ability – much to the relief of many teachers, and, in some instances, after pressure from the teaching community. The general feeling amongst English teachers is that English and English literature are subjects in which students can be encouraged to demonstrate their knowledge and understanding without recourse to these methods. In the main, therefore, differention is achieved by outcome, both in coursework and in written examinations.

CONCLUDING COMMENTS AND FUTURE PROSPECTS

The GCSE criteria for English support many positive initiatives in English teaching. The view of English expressed in the criteria is one which encourages teachers to see their students as active users and interpreters of language, able to use their language resources to communicate confidently with others, to respond sensitively to what they hear and read, and to be critically aware of how language is used by others. There are, of course, aspects of English which many teachers would see as central to their subject that are absent from the criteria. For instance, although the criteria (Section A, para. 1.3) do recognize the ability of students to 'understand themselves and others' as one of the aims of English courses, there is little explicit mention otherwise of the wider social aspects of studying English – of how, for example, literary and non-literary texts express the prevailing social and ideological values of the times in which they are produced, or of the means by which the study of literature can be used to gain insights into the workings of the society in which students live.

It is too soon to judge how far the potential inherent in the criteria for effecting positive change in the English curriculum will be realized. For example, in the case of oral work in the classroom, it is likely to take years for the inertia of a system which has valued literacy at the expense of 'oracy' since its inception to be overcome.

Much will depend, too, on how Examining Groups respond to the initiatives which will continue to develop now that the GCSE is under way. Many of these initiatives are likely to come from teachers, using the potential of coursework to explore new and stimulating ways of teaching English. We have yet to see quite what impact the grade-related criteria will have upon the subject.

Other, more pragmatic conditions will also have to be satisfied if the potential inherent in the new courses is to be fully realized. For, as with many other subjects, GCSE courses in English need additional resources if students are to be given the wider and more rewarding learning experiences envisaged by the criteria. These resources include not only the provision of books, audio-visual equipment and software, artwork materials, funding for out-of-school activities and the like, but most importantly, adequate in-service provision. GCSE English presents many challenges to teachers, who will need the opportunity to gain experience and benefit from the ideas of others.

REFERENCES

Barnes, D. and Seed, J. (1981) *Seals of Approval: An Analysis of English Examinations*, University of Leeds School of Education, Leeds

Knight, R. (1985) Speaking out, *Times Educational Supplement*, 6 September

National Association for the Teaching of English (1980) *Coursework in English: Principles and Assessments* (NATE Examinations Booklet No. 3), NATE, Huddersfield

Scott, P. (1983) *Coursework in English: Seven Case Studies*, Longmans, York

Chapter 8
MATHEMATICS
Christine Shiu (*Open University*)

The teaching of mathematics in schools has been the focus of much notice in recent years. Attention has been drawn to:

1 what is taught – and its appropriateness;
2 how it is taught – and the effectiveness of that teaching;
3 the standards attained – and how these are to be measured.

A major influence on all of these aspects is acknowledged to be the system of public examinations in mathematics especially O-level and CSE. The development of GCSE examinations in mathematics therefore provides a major opportunity for deliberately affecting the teaching and learning of mathematics in schools.

THE COMMITTEE OF INQUIRY

Mathematics teaching became subject to particularly close scrutiny at the time of the 'great debate' in the 1970s, when questions were raised about the nature and purpose of mathematics education. In October 1976 the newly formed Assessment of Performance Unit (APU) began work and in 1980 produced its first secondary survey of mathematics. The news (APU, 1980) that only 35 per cent of the fifteen-year olds sampled could correctly evaluate '$40 \div 0.8 =$ ' was taken by some to mean that the basics were being neglected (despite the fact that the success rates for '$1.8 \div 3 =$ ' and '$396 \div 6 =$ ' were respectively 66 per cent and 82 per cent), whereas others thought the whole issue of what mathematics was taught to whom was thrown into question by this response. Further evidence (Hart, 1981) was produced at about the same time at Chelsea College, University of London, by the Concepts in Secondary Mathematics and Science (CSMS) team. They reported that some 30 per cent of the same age group asserted that '$8 \times 0.4 =$' gives a greater answer than '$8 \div 0.4 =$', apparently believing that 'multiplication (always) makes bigger' and 'division' (always) makes smaller', and thus demonstrating that they had made a sensible, if not accurate, generalization based on their mathematical experience. It seemed clear that whilst APU might produce evidence about the effects of current mathematics teaching, it was no part of their task to predict what the effects of changes in practice might be. Against this background the government decided to set up a Committee of Inquiry into all aspects of the teaching of mathematics, with particular emphasis on the mathematical needs of adult life. The committee published its report under the title *Mathematics Counts* (Cockcroft, 1982).

Early responses included: the mounting of courses by LEAs and organizations such as the Mathematical Association to disseminate its recommendations; and then the production of documents by various bodies such as *Teaching Styles – a Response to Cockcroft 243* by the Association of Teachers of Mathematics (ATM, 1984). Its influence on the subsequent DES document *Mathematics from 5 to 16* was considerable, and it is probably the document which most influenced the SEC in its production of criteria for mathematics. Indeed criterion 1.2 of the *National Criteria for Mathematics* states that:

> When devising examinations in mathematics regard should be paid to the discussion and recommendations to be found in the Report of the Committee of Inquiry into the Teaching of Mathematics in schools (the Cockcroft Report). Of especial importance is the statement that 'pupils must not be required to prepare for examinations which are not suited to their attainment nor must these examinations be of a kind which will undermine the confidence of pupils'. (SEC, 1985a)

THE COCKCROFT REPORT

The Cockcroft Report addresses four major questions which have a direct bearing on assessment at 16+, and which therefore underpin a number of points made in both the *National Criteria for Mathematics* and the *Draft Grade Criteria*, These are:

1 Why teach mathematics?
2 What mathematics should be taught to whom?
3 How may mathematics be taught most effectively?
4 How should mathematics be examined?

These are examined in turn.

Why teach mathematics?

The opening chapter considers the aims of teaching mathematics and supports the traditional view that mathematics is an essential component of the education of all children throughout the years of compulsory schooling. The reasons for this are formulated mainly in terms of its usefulness in everyday life, in other school subjects, and in science and technology, and in its power as a means of communication. However, the intrinsic rewards of studying mathematics are also acknowledged in the discussion of the aim 'of helping each pupil to develop so far as is possible his appreciation and enjoyment of mathematics itself'. Sadly the evidence of their own commissioned survey of the use of mathematics by adults in daily life reveals only too clearly how little that aim has been realized in the past.

What mathematics should be taught to whom?

When considering what mathematics should be taught Cockcroft points out that most mathematics syllabuses used in secondary schools have evolved from those designed for pupils in the top quarter of the ability range, and are often too difficult for the majority of pupils. The report states very strongly that it considers this a wrong approach, and recommends that:

> [. . .] development should be 'from the bottom upwards' by considering the range of work which is appropriate for lower-attaining pupils and extending this range as the level of attainment of pupils increases.

Furthermore:

> We believe it should be a fundamental principle that no topic should be included unless it can be developed sufficiently for it to be applied in ways which the pupils can understand.

These are admirable if somewhat revolutionary principles in the light of current and previous practice. Even if they are accepted not everyone will agree as to what is that appropriate range of work or what topics are capable of sufficient development by pupils. It will be some time before these issues are clarified though some clues may be derived from the previously mentioned APU and CSMS data.

Nevertheless the report does set out a foundation list of mathematics topics which are considered appropriate for pupils in about the lowest 40 per cent of the range of attainment in mathematics. In discussing courses for the highest 60 per cent, two reference levels are prescribed. It is suggested that pupils who achieve around CSE grade 4 under the present system (and who are therefore likely to achieve GCSE grade F) should not tackle a syllabus much greater than the foundation list; whereas syllabuses for the top 20 per cent should be similar to O-level ones. Also that there should be another examination syllabus with content lying between that of the two reference levels, giving a total of three levels. This is justified by the committee's belief that the better matching of course content to levels of attainment and rates of learning will lead to greater confidence in approaches to mathematics and greater mastery of the mathematics studied, and thus to an overall raising of standards. However many teachers will feel that our current system already forces premature choices in mathematics teaching, and that even more differentiation of courses may exacerbate this.

How may mathematics be taught most effectively?

The Cockcroft Report goes on to probe the teaching of mathematics in schools in the light of its identified aims. It considers the nature of mathematical knowledge, and examines what is meant by understanding mathematics, and how a teacher can recognize and develop such understanding. The role of memory, and the appropriateness of rote learning in mathematics, are discussed, leading to a consideration of teaching methods.

The DES publication *Aspects of Secondary Education in England* reports that in many of the schools surveyed much mathematics teaching lacked variety, and consisted only of exposition by the teacher and individually worked practice examples by the children. This was particularly true of children of lower mathematical ability. However, Cockcroft states that mathematics teaching at all levels should also include discussion, practical work, problem-solving and investigational work. What exactly do these new components mean in terms of mathematics?

Since these are generally less widespread, they may need explanation as well as justification. Much of the power of mathematics resides in its ability to express concepts and relationships concisely and unambiguously; however, many people have much difficulty in acquiring and using this power. Most, if not all, children require extensive practice in articulating and refining their mathematical ideas orally before this can be achieved. It follows that discussion is an essential component of both mathematics teaching and learning. A similar justification exists for the use of practical materials. Many abstract mathematical ideas arose originally from practical situations and the need to solve practical problems. Thus for many learners concepts can be developed, and new situations better envisaged, through the handling of practical materials. On the other hand, mathematicians throughout history have worked to preserve the coherence and consistency of the body of knowledge which is known as mathematics. It is through the investigation of patterns and relationships that children can come to appreciate and handle this aspect of mathematics.

If however teaching is entirely expository and teachers present mathematical structures only as finished systems of definitions and procedures, such structures frequently appear to children as random and arbitrary. They develop no notion that mathematics has evolved by a mixture of invention and discovery on the part of ordinary human beings. They have no confidence in their own power to engage in mathematical thinking and become convinced that they need to be taught the rules.

For the reasons outlined above, the full variety of teaching styles is necessary for a more stable understanding of mathematics, with a richer supporting structure of associations and images, and a greater confidence in handling mathematical ideas than is usually evidenced by many adults in our society. However, describing ideal classroom practice does not, in itself, tell us how to measure its outcomes. The question must be faced as to how the desired understanding and confidence is to be assessed.

How should mathematics be examined?

The mathematical learning achieved by pupils as the result of purely expository teaching can be satisfactorily measured by written terminal examinations. However the ability to investigate mathematical ideas independently cannot be assessed by the kind of questions which can be answered in an examination room in very limited time. This is acknowledged by Cockcroft, who suggests that (a) other modes of assessment will be required in addition to the traditional one and (b) these will involve the direct participation of the class teacher. These two proposals although in accordance with the general criteria for GCSE depart radically from customary practice in GCE mathematics, in which it is usual for all assessment to be carried out by written examination papers which are set and marked by examination boards and not by teachers. It is the involvement of teachers in the assessment of their own students which may well have the most profound effect on classroom practice, and which is likely to have immense impact on the relationship between teacher and pupils.

In the next section the *National Criteria for Mathematics* (SEC, 1985a), and the *Draft Grade Criteria* (SEC, 1985b) are examined to see how far they reflect the Cockcroft recommendations and enable their implementation.

THE NATIONAL CRITERIA FOR MATHEMATICS AND THE DRAFT GRADE CRITERIA

The *National Criteria for Mathematics* are unique in that they need to take full account of a recent major report commissioned by government as well as meet the general criteria. The need to establish grade criteria was set in the mathematics criteria when these outlined what criteria must be satisfied by candidates who are awarded grades C and F.

Aims

The Cockcroft aims for teaching mathematics are implicit in the introduction to the National Criteria which sets out guidelines for the interpretation of the criteria which follow. Any scheme of assessment will include among other aspects the assessment of 'pupils' understanding of mathematical processes in the solution of problems and their ability to reason mathematically'. It will also enable pupils 'to demonstrate what they know and can do rather than what they do not know or cannot do' and 'to develop their knowledge and understanding of mathematics to the full extent of their capabilities, to have experience of mathematics as a means of solving practical problems and to develop confidence in their use of mathematics' and provide 'examination tasks to relate [. . .] to the use of mathematics in everyday situations'.

The introduction also acknowledges the considerable influence which mathematics examinations at 16+ exert on the content and pace of work in secondary classrooms. It is therefore considered essential 'that syllabuses and methods of assessment for these examinations should not conflict with the provision and development of appropriate and worthwhile mathematics courses in schools'.

Further guidance as to what appropriate and worthwhile courses might involve is offered in the *Draft Grade Criteria*, which begin by identifying two distinct domains, covering the aspects of mathematics considered relevant to secondary schoolchildren. The first domain consists of concepts, skills and procedures, and their use in solving problems of standard types which can be recognized by the pupils. 'It includes routine aspects of mental, oral, written and practical work together with the use of calculators and of measuring and drawing instruments of various kinds.' The second domain comprises strategy, implementation and communication and 'encompasses the abilities of pupils to formulate and interpret problems, develop strategies for their solution, identify and collect necessary data and information, make use of relevant mathematical concepts and skills, evaluate and interpret results, draw conclusions and communicate these by oral, written or graphical methods. It is also concerned with the ability to reason logically and, at the higher grade levels, with the ability to work with abstract ideas, to generalise and to prove'.

Thus the Cockcroft emphasis on the power of mathematics as a means of communication and the objective of sharing that power with all pupils to the extent to which they are capable is taken up and endorsed by both sets of criteria. Furthermore when discussing the assessment of the second domain the *Draft Grade Criteria* state:

> Whatever the means of assessment there should be a balance both in the types of activities which are assessed and in their mathematical coverage [. . .] Starting points should, where possible, be taken from the world of the pupil and tasks should involve some realistic purpose or application. This does not however, mean that pure mathematical investigations should be excluded; these can often engage the interest of pupils of all levels of attainment and so make a valuable contribution to mathematical development. Pupils should be encouraged on occasion to initiate their own tasks and to relate them to their work in other subjects. (SEC, 1985b)

In other words, the relating of mathematics to real-life situations, and to other school subjects, is reiterated but modified with the proviso 'where possible', and the reference to the potential interest of all pupils in pure investigations invokes the appreciation and enjoyment of mathematics for its own sake.

Content

Examining first the National Criteria reveals that they take up the Cockcroft recommendation of differentiation, with a specific criterion reading:

> 4.1 In any differentiated scheme offering the full range of grades there will normally be at least three levels of assessment. For each of these a separate content must be prescribed. This will consist of 'core' items, common to the syllabuses of all Examining Groups, together with additional material chosen at the discretion of the Group devising the syllabus. The 'core' items are set out in List 1 and List 2 below.

List 1 corresponds quite closely to the Cockcroft foundation list, and therefore carries forward the assumption that indeed these are topics which will allow the development of a 'bottom-up' curriculum. List 2 adds those items necessary to any syllabus which can lead to the award of a grade C. Examining groups must choose additional material to provide 'a syllabus well in excess of that contained in List 1 and List 2' for pupils aspiring to the award of grades A or B.

Both lists are formulated in terms which relate to domain 1. The abilities which are included in domain 2 are not tied to any particular content since they are sufficiently general to apply to a wide range of content. It is of course necessary to provide some content for them to be demonstrated, but the wording of the National Criteria allows for almost unlimited choice of that content with only the caveat that 'where a coursework element is offered' this must be 'complementary to, and not a duplicate of, written examination papers'.

Teaching styles

Most of the 17 assessment objectives listed in the criteria relate to familiar abilities, and do not in themselves imply changes in teaching style, however the final two are signalled as distinctive:

> Two further assessment objectives can be fully realised only by assessing work carried out by candidates in addition to time-limited written examinations. From 1988 to 1990 all Examining Groups must provide at least one scheme which includes some elements of these two objectives. From 1991 these objectives must be realised fully in all schemes.

These objectives are:

> 3.16 respond orally to questions about mathematics, discuss mathematical ideas and carry out mental calculations;

> 3.17 carry out practical and investigational work, and undertake extended pieces of work.

These two criteria relate directly to the teaching styles recommended in Cockcroft and thus it is hoped will encourage their adoption. Further, schools and examining bodies need to develop assessment procedures to meet them.

Assessment

Criterion 3.16 certainly seems to imply that formal assessment will include an oral component. What it does not specify is whether that aspect can be assessed incidentally, perhaps within the course of a normal mathematics lesson, in which case it would be entirely within the scope of responsibility of the regular class teacher; or whether a specific event must be arranged for oral assessment, such as exists for foreign languages. Also should the assessment be carried out within a group situation, or is it more fittingly a one to one exchange between assessor and candidate?

Similar questions arise with practical work and its assessment. One possible approach would be individual interviews of the type developed by the APU in its practical testing programme. However it should be remembered that these were used to survey a small sample of the relevant population, and that testing every examination candidate in this way might not prove to be feasible.

It is not even certain that it is desirable. In the classroom investigation, practical work and discussion are not separable activities. Rather discussion and practical work are tools in the clarification of concepts and the understanding of problems, and perhaps can only be treated as such. The testing of process aspects of mathematics is only in its infancy and many questions remain to be resolved. The *Draft Grade Criteria* set out behaviours to be exhibited by candidates at different grades, with respect to domain 2, but themselves acknowledge that their attribution of these to particular levels was necessarily based on judgement rather than evidence. It is essential that these issues are left open so that various interpretations may be used and tested.

The National Criteria simply state that:

> Coursework may take a variety of forms including practical and investigational work; tasks should be appropriate to candidates' individual levels of ability.

One of the purposes of the working party which produced the *Draft Grade Criteria* was to make more explicit what characteristics such appropriate tasks might possess. Having identified the two domains, they set out possible criteria for the assessment of work in domain 2, and acknowledge the possibility of applying different criteria to similar kinds of work submitted by pupils of different levels of ability. This might also imply different modes of assessment for such work. For example, under the criteria for interpretation and communication, the pupil at grade F will have to:

> [. . .] explain orally or in writing, the problem, the strategy used and the outcome incorporating, where appropriate, visual forms of presentation including tables, diagrams, charts or models.

Whereas the pupil at grade C will in addition demonstrate the ability to:

> [. . .] present results in an orderly sequence, orally or in writing, using an adequate range of mathematical language and symbols and incorporating appropriate visual forms, including graphs.

And to achieve an A grade it will be necessary for the pupil to:

[. . .] give a clear account of the task, verbally or in writing, giving reasons for the strategies used and explaining assumptions or simplifications which have been made; select the most appropriate method of communicating results, making effective use of a range of mathematical language and notations, diagrams, charts, graphs and computer output.

Whoever has control of this part of the assessment may well decide that oral assessment is appropriate for the grade F student, whereas it is more fitting (or convenient) for the grade A student to present a written report. Whether or not this decision will be in the hands of the classroom teacher, it is clear that many aspects of the implementation of the new forms of assessment will have considerable impact on classroom practice. Just what form this impact will take is considered in the next section.

IMPLICATIONS FOR CLASSROOM PRACTICE

Most teachers would find themselves able to agree with the aims of mathematics teaching set out by Cockcroft. However this agreement does not at present lead to uniformity of practice. Although there are mathematics classrooms in which teaching styles and learning activities encompass the advocated variety, there remain many, where in the words of *Aspects of Secondary Education in England*:

[. . .] the ideas of the course need to be shown in a broader setting with more attention to the relevance of mathematics [. . .] (and) [. . .] pupils need opportunities to undertake more independent work [. . .]. (DES, 1979)

These will need to undergo profound changes. In particular in schools where the emphasis has been on individual work usually carried out in silence, a new emphasis on group work, use of practical materials, and discussion may need considerable adaptation on the part of both teachers and pupils. Such profound changes in behaviour cannot easily be acquired in the one or two years of schooling prior to the 16+ examination, and so pupils will ideally experience variety in mathematics learning throughout their school careers. This is the major reason for not making the coursework requirement compulsory in mathematics until 1991. It will give to schools not yet operating in this way, the opportunity to develop new courses with eleven-year-olds entering secondary education in 1986. Even given this time-scale many teachers will need considerable in-service support within their schools. A possible basis for a department to begin its own in-service provision might be the OU video-tape *Secondary Mathematics : Classroom Practice* which was commissioned by the DES to illustrate investigation, discussion and practical work in the mathematics classroom.

Changes in practice will also give rise to a number of practical problems which may also need to be solved on a departmental basis. A specific concern of the Cockcroft Report was the impact of calculators and computers on the mathematics classroom. Surprisingly, computers are not mentioned in the National Criteria, though the use of electronic calculators is listed amongst the assessment objectives. However the *Draft Grade Criteria*, published in September 1985, do require pupils to make use of a range of resources including calculators and computers, at all grade levels; this is a requirement which is likely to persist in future versions of such criteria. This may well have a resource implication for some schools who may need both to develop a policy for the use of calculators and computers throughout the curriculum, and provide sufficient quantities for use by their students. It is worth pointing out that the Cockcroft Report says explicitly:

[. . .] we recommend that steps should be taken, perhaps by means of a scheme similar to that for providing micro-computers in secondary schools, to ensure that the necessary calculators are available in secondary schools as soon as possible and in any case not later than 1985.

At the time of writing this recommendation has not been implemented.

Calculators and computers are (significant) among those materials which may be used in the mathematics classroom in attempts to implement practical work, though many other (more or less expensive) items will be identified as either necessary, or desirable. Once these are obtained, how and where are they to be stored, and how is access to them to be gained most effectively?

Attention will also need to be paid to the allocation of time within both mathematics lessons and courses. As well as replanning the timing of the introduction of specific content there will be a number of new questions to be addressed. How much time should be devoted to the production of extended pieces of work? If the teacher is to conduct either individual, or group orals, or practical sessions, as part of the assessment, how much of his or her usual teaching time will be taken up by this; and who will have responsibility for the rest of this class during these sessions?

Another issue which all teachers of examination classes will face is the one which arises from the requirement on the boards to produce differentiated courses. Currently teachers and pupils are faced with a twofold choice between GCE and CSE entry, with the possibility of double entry for borderline candidates. It appears that differentiated syllabuses will enforce a threefold choice, with no possibility of double-entering. In these circumstances a wrong decision may well have disastrous consequences if a pupil fails to meet the criteria for the lowest grade catered for by their choice of entry and is consequently left without any grade at all. Furthermore until teachers are accustomed to the new system, there may be a significant number of wrong decisions made.

However, decisions about levels of entry may become easier from one point of view. If students have completed some of their coursework before final entries are made, then its quality could become an appropriate indicator of their likely final grade. Indeed the *Draft Grade Criteria* for domain 2 quoted earlier can be taken to imply an alternative version of differentiation, in which the same starting point, or situation, is explored at different levels rather than giving pupils of differing abilities different starting points. Teachers of younger children often use this approach, and it may be possible to develop it for use in fourth and fifth forms. It would be very exciting if syllabuses embodying this notion were to be devised and approved, and then used by committed teachers.

THE FUTURE

It is clear that only as the new GCSE syllabuses and examinations are implemented will their impact become manifest. Examining Groups under the aegis of the SEC will attempt to apply the National Criteria in approving these syllabuses; and that as these syllabuses are used their effect and the effectiveness of the criteria in carrying out the Cockroft recommendations, will be seen.

The outstanding questions would appear to be the following:

What will the testing of practical and oral skills in mathematics come to mean in practice, and will this testing give pupils the hoped-for opportunities to show what they can do and understand in mathematics?

What difference will the involvement of the teacher in formal assessment make to his or her role and relationship with his or her pupils?

Will the changes in assessment procedures bring about the kind of classroom practices advocated by Cockcroft?

Finally – and most important of all – will those changes lead to greater confidence, enjoyment and achievement in mathematics by the pupils in our schools?

REFERENCES

APU (1980)*Mathematical Development: Secondary Survey Report No. 1*, HMSO, London

ATM (1984) *Teaching Styles – Response to Cockcroft 243*, Association of Teachers of Mathematics, Derby

DES (1979) *Aspects of Secondary Education in England*, HMSO, London

DES (1982) *Mathematics Counts – Report of the Committee of Inquiry into the Teaching of Mathematics under the Chairmanship of Dr W. H. Cockcroft*, HMSO, London

DES (1985) *Mathematics from 5 to 16*, Curriculum Matters 3 – an HMI series, HMSO, London

Hart K. (ed.) (1981) *Children's Understanding of Mathematics 11–16*, John Murray, London

Open University (1985) *Secondary Mathematics: Classroom Practice*, from Learning Materials Service, PO Box 188, Milton Keynes MK7 6DH

SEC (1985a) *National Criteria for Mathematics*, Secondary Examinations Council, London

SEC (1985b) *Draft Grade Criteria – Report of Mathematics Working Party*, Secondary Examinations Council, London

Chapter 9
SCIENCE
Barbara Hodgson (*Open University*)

HOPES AND FEARS

The transition to science under GCSE has been welcomed by many – including, importantly, the Association for Science Education (1985). Prospectively this transition will provide the stimulus for curricula changes towards the aims of those concerned with improving science education as well as to significant, and positive, changes in the assessment of the science subjects.

How will the new examination system affect the science curriculum in schools? The two most important changes stem from the strengthening of the link between process and content, and the shift in emphasis from mere recall of knowledge to its understanding and application. The *National Criteria*, Science (DES, 1985b, Section 6) require that not less than 20 per cent of the total available marks are to be allocated to the assessment of experimental and other practical skills. Syllabus developers have to limit the content of syllabuses so that enough time is available for the development of competence in scientific processes. As techniques for the assessment of experimental skills are developed and broadened, more opportunities for introducing problem-solving activities will be possible. An increased emphasis on technological applications and social and economic issues should lead to greater understanding of the use, applications, and limitations of science.

Changes in assessment are signalled by the major aim of the GCSE to provide a positive assessment experience for everyone. All candidates must have the opportunity to show 'what they know, understand and can do'. In science, this means that differential schemes of assessment are necessary.

All candidates are required to solve problems using the methods of science, reflecting the increased emphasis on process and understanding, and the reduced importance given to straight recall. Another major change for many science teachers is the introduction of an element of coursework assessment. In science, this has initially been equated with the assessment of practical and experimental skills, and at least half of the assessment of experimental skills must be carried out during the course by the teacher.

The transition to a new system of assessment is unlikely to be plain sailing. The gains may well be costly, many believe the vessel could founder very quickly. If the GCSE in science is to be implemented successfully, problems of resource, technique, and timescale need to be resolved. Given current staff–student ratios, coursework assessment of experimental skills may prove an intolerable extra burden. The ever-increasing problem of insufficient equipment, and laboratory space, also has to be faced. Teachers will have to develop and practice new skills and techniques of assessment while also implementing other changes in their teaching. They will, therefore, need extra time to assimilate these changes, and to meet the new demands that are being made on them. Not everyone will experience the same, or all of these difficulties, but the timescale and resources for the transition must appear woefully inadequate to those faced with these problems.

THE NATIONAL CRITERIA AND THE SCIENCE CURRICULUM

Content

Four sets of criteria covering science were published in 1985. The National Criteria for science (DES, 1985b) define the essentials for all GCSE courses in the broad field of experimentally based science but provide no syllabus content. The other three sets of criteria cover the separate science subjects of biology (DES, 1985c), chemistry (DES, 1985d), and physics (DES, 1985e). These criteria conform to the National Criteria for science (DES, 1985b) and also specify a core content in the relevant subject area.

For some time teachers and examiners (and no doubt students also) have been concerned about the ever-expanding content of science courses. Recognizing this, the criteria offer guidelines to limit the amount of knowledge required. The criteria for biology, chemistry and physics specify a core content and allow for the addition of up to, but no more than, half as much material again. However, it is not necessary to add to the core content of all – syllabuses may be designed to promote a deeper treatment and understanding of the core rather than coverage of further topics. In addition, the criteria for the separate science subjects require a reasonably even coverage of the core content and an assessment that reflects this coverage.

Content may also be reduced by the need to avoid overlap with other subjects. Section 19 of the General Criteria for the GCSE (DES, 1985a) deals with the proliferation of subject titles. A subject title must give a clear indication of the nature and content of the subject, and it must cover an area of subject content distinct from that of other recognized subject titles. Any title accepted must be broad enough to cover the range of subject content likely to be included in different syllabuses in the same subject area.

Process

The first stated aim of the National Criteria for science (DES, 1985b, para. 2.1) is 'to provide through well designed studies of experimental and practical science a worthwhile educational experience for all pupils whether or not they go on to study science beyond this level'. Many science process skills are included in the assessment objectives, and some of these objectives relate specifically to experimental aspects of scientific investigation and study.

There may be some confusion between the terms 'practical' and 'experimental'. It is important to be clear as to what is meant by them. It is fairly obvious from the assessment objectives which areas of activity are intended. Practical skills and techniques, such as observing and making measurements in biology, selecting and manipulating appropriate apparatus in chemistry, or connecting electrical circuits in physics are needed to conduct experiments, but do not individually constitute experiments. Equally, there are abilities which are needed for the successful conduct of any experimental enquiry but which are not practical in the sense defined above. These include the ability to plan, modify, interpret and report on experiments.

Thus the processes of experimental science are included for assessment in the National Criteria for science. All candidates are required to devise and carry out experimental tests for particular purposes, such as checking the validity of data, conclusions and generalizations. In so doing, they have to select suitable apparatus and use it effectively and safely. There is a further emphasis on safety in the requirement that students be able to follow instructions accurately so that experiments are carried out safely.

However, science is not only about carrying out experiments. Doing science (thinking and exploring scientifically) involves a variety of intellectual skills, processes and abilities which are not solely part of the experimental process. These science process skills figure prominently in the National Criteria for science (DES, 1985b, para. 3.2) and include the ability to translate information from one form to another; to extract from available information data relevant to a particular context; to apply scientific methods and ideas in problem-solving situations; to recognize patterns, form hypotheses, and deduce relationships when working with experimental data; and to make decisions based on the examination of evidence and arguments. These intellectual processes and experimental skills are implicit in most GCE and CSE courses but now they are explicitly to be assessed. Consequently, time and attention should be given to their development.

Another recent influence on the science curriculum is underlined by the GCSE criteria. This is the importance of the relationship between the content and the contexts of science and the need to present the study of science in a way that relates to issues seen as important by young people. The General Criteria (DES, 1985a, para. 19) stipulate that candidates should have a chance to understand the relationship of a subject to other areas of study, and its relevance to their own lives. The National Criteria for science respond to this requirement by stating that 'at least 15 per cent of the total marks are to be allocated to assessments relating to technical applications and social, economic, and environmental issues', with particular emphasis being given to technological applications. This requirement is paralleled in the subject-specific criteria, and in chemistry some specific, though fairly broad, guidance about suitable topics for the study of applications, and social and economic implications are included in the core content. For some teachers this will be new, but there is experience to be drawn upon in projects such as the Association for Science Education's Science and Technology in Society projects – SATIS (Association for Science Education, in preparation).

Two further stipulations in the General Criteria (DES, 1985a) that need careful consideration are those concerning avoidance of bias, and recognition of cultural diversity. Syllabuses and examinations, and by implication, classroom teaching, should be free of political, ethnic, gender, and other forms of bias. Examiners and teachers are also asked to incorporate materials which reflect the cultural diversity of society.

GCSE ASSESSMENT IN SCIENCE

The innovative features of assessment in the GCSE stem from a philosophy that aims to make assessment a positive experience for everyone. The General Criteria (DES, 1985a, para. 16) require that candidates across the entire ability range must be given 'opportunities to demonstrate their knowledge, abilities and achievements: that is to show what they know, understand and can do'. This means that in all subjects it is necessary to provide for differentiation either through differentiated papers, or through differentiated questions within papers.

The National Criteria for science ensure that, in syllabuses for which the whole range of grades can be awarded, differentiated schemes of assessment involve alternative components for different levels of attainment. The biology (DES, 1985c), chemistry (DES, 1985d), and physics (DES, 1985e) criteria all stipulate that schemes applicable over the full grade range should have alternative papers pitched at different levels of difficulty. The National Criteria for physics (DES, 1985e) face up to the inevitable problem in stating that it would be extremely difficult, if a scheme of entirely common papers were adopted, to provide GCSE physics examination papers which 'would be challenging to the whole candidature and which would discriminate reliably across the full grade range.' (DES, 1985e, para. 6.4)

There are a variety of possible structures for a scheme using differentiated papers. Some have a common component taken by all candidates; others do not. It appears that the majority of science syllabuses will adopt the common paper plus extension paper model, with the common paper covering abilities up to say grade C and the more difficult extension paper extending the available grade range to A.

It will be a considerable challenge in science subjects to define tasks, and set questions, that can be tackled successfully at all levels of attainment. In written papers, the familiar kinds of tasks, and methods of discrimination, are likely to be used, but these must be evaluated carefully to ensure that they make the required contribution to GCSE assessment schemes. Some limits have been placed on the use of different types of tasks. For instance, not more than two-thirds of marks on the written papers of an examination can be allocated to objective tests and some extended prose writing must be included.

Assessment objectives in science apply across the whole ability range so therefore all students must have the opportunity not only to practice and demonstrate specific scientific knowledge and skills but also to apply scientific ideas and methods in the solution of qualitative and quantitative problems. In a differentiated scheme, teachers have an additional responsibility to guide students to aim for the most appropriate levels of attainment. Teachers therefore need to be familiar with the demands made by all components of the assessment scheme.

COURSEWORK ASSESSMENT IN SCIENCE

The problems associated with changes to written examinations are mainly the province of those responsible for providing the examinations. The assessment change which most directly affects teachers is the introduction of coursework assessment. The General Criteria call for an element of school- or centre-assessed coursework, and in science subjects this requirement tends immediately to be equated with the assessment of experimental skills in the laboratory.

What is expected?

The National Criteria for science suggest that assessment through coursework should be chosen when this is the most appropriate means of assessing objectives. Obviously, objectives relating to the safe handling of apparatus, instruments and chemicals, or to the planning and execution of extended scientific investigations do not lend themselves to assessment in timed written papers. Coursework can, however, take whatever form is appropriate, and can include written, practical or oral assignments. It can be assessed either periodically or continuously and can take place during any part or throughout the duration of the course. Projects are recognized as an important form of coursework and allow higher order skills such as synthesis, evaluation and problem-solving to be assessed. A project can have many forms – for example, a case study, an experimental investigation in the laboratory, or in the field, or the design and construction of an artefact. Project work could provide a relevant sphere in which to assess the technological application of the scientific content of a course. However, the National Criteria for science do appear to constrain the range of coursework used for assessment purposes. Section 6.4 states that 'All schemes of assessment must allocate not less than 20 per cent of the total marks to experimental and other practical skills', and at least half this 20 per cent must be awarded 'on the basis of experimental and observational work in the laboratory or its equivalent'.

How will it be done?

In planning for coursework assessment, the work to be assessed should be able to arise naturally in any teaching and learning scheme. One of the advantages of coursework assessment is that it does not have the 'sudden death' aspect of timed written examinations. This advantage is lost if the assessment is concentrated in the few months immediately before the written papers. The experimental work associated with any course has to be planned to allow development of experimental and practical skills and assessment of such skills at regular intervals.

GCSE syllabuses in science subjects include advice to teachers on how to carry out such assessments. This advice may range from a totally prescribed system to general advice with suggestions for suitable tasks. For example, one scheme suggests that six specified practical skills should each be assessed three times during a two-year course. Suggestions are given as to suitable tasks and criteria for the assessment of levels of attainment are provided. A rather different scheme proposes that 10 per cent of marks should be awarded for school-based competency tests of basic practical skills. A list of test options is provided for teachers, and candidates can be assessed as often as they like and the best mark achieved can be submitted. Higher-level experimental skills would be assessed in a longer practical test set by the Examining Group.

Whatever the mechanics of the scheme, the choice of tasks offered for assessment is extremely important. As with written examination questions, tasks must be applicable across the whole ability range, so allowing all candidates to show what they can do. For basic skills such as reading information from graphs, tables and charts, following instructions and performing basic observations, and measurement and interpretation tasks the concept of mastery or proficiency is emerging quite strongly. As all candidates are expected to be able to master such basic tasks, differentiation may be largely unnecessary. More complex situations designed to assess higher order skills give more scope for differentiated tasks.

Many syllabus planners think that the work of the Assessment of Performance Unit (APU) provides a useful basis for defining practical assessment objectives, and the practical and experimental skills listed for assessment are often closely linked to the APU skills categories (APU, 1985a, 1985b). This kind of coursework assessment is new to many, but much useful exploratory and pilot work has been done by the Examining Groups, by projects such as the Oxford Certificate of Educational Achievement (OCEA, 1985) and the Graded Assessment in Science Project (GASP, 1985) as well as the APU. These projects provide an invaluable fund of ideas for assessable experimental tasks.

Finding suitable tasks is not the only problem. Management and organizational issues must also be considered. In some examination centres, assessment takes place in large classes and ways have to be found to ensure that everyone has an equal opportunity to be assessed without assessment swamping the practical work of the course. Difficulties may also occur in determining an individual's contribution to a group exercise, or project, and in assessing extended investigations. Equipment scarcity could be a problem and so could staff or student absence. None of these issues is irresolvable, but careful planning will be necessary.

Assessing to criteria

Those responsible for coursework assessment need clear performance criteria if they are to assess the attainment of their students against a set of national standards. The National Criteria for science rightly insist that standards applied in coursework assessment must always be those which apply in the final examination, regardless of when the assessment is made. As syllabuses are likely to allow coursework assessment at almost any time throughout a two-year course, a clear description of the quality of work expected at various levels of attainment at 16+ is needed.

Performance criteria for practical and experimental skills in science are being presented in a variety of ways. They may be related to a particular assessment objective, or group of objectives, and describe an overall performance on that objective. Those objectives relating to the use and organization of apparatus, for instance, can have descriptions of performance where criteria at the top of the attainment range include 'assembles and organizes apparatus with dexterity and confidence' and at the bottom 'can use individual pieces of apparatus adequately'. Another approach is to specify individual criteria within a broad objective such as 'designing simple experiments to solve problems', to suggest rating scales for these and in addition to describe overall performances expected for, say, three particular grades, leaving assessors to interpolate for other grades. Assessment criteria may be linked to suitable tasks, or it may be left to the coursework assessor to match tasks appropriate to the course to the criteria provided.

MORE CHANGES?

Yet further changes to the teaching and learning of science are likely to take place in the next few years. Following hard on the heels of the GCSE subject criteria are further sets of criteria, known as grade-related criteria, which define what candidates must do to be awarded each particular grade in a subject. The large numbers of individual criteria which could be required have been grouped into domains. The current suggestion is that biology, chemistry and physics should have the same three domains, namely:

1　knowledge and understanding;
2　handling information and problem-solving;
3　practical skills and investigating.

It is possible that even more emphasis – up to one third of the available marks – will be put on experimental and practical skills and this will no doubt extend the amount of coursework assessment. Also, it seems likely that candidates will be graded in each domain, thus providing a fuller account of their competency and moving towards a record of achievement rather than a single grade.

Another major question is whether science in schools will continue in its present form as several separate subjects. The DES/Welsh Office (1985) policy statement *Science 5–16: A Statement of Policy*, calls for breadth and balance in science education. To achieve this within the time likely to be provided for science in the curriculum suggests a need to reduce the three traditional separate sciences into something two-thirds the size. One obvious solution has been a double-award scheme of integrated science. With the advent of the GCSE, perhaps schemes of combined science will emerge. The National Criteria for science define combined science as 'a multicomponent area of study wherein the syllabuses, in the teaching and in the examination the components are, as far as practicable, mutually supportive while retaining much of their separate identities'. The recognition of scientific skills and processes common to all areas and the reduction in required core content certainly seem to make such an outcome possible.

Whatever the immediate and longer-term changes, it is to be hoped that GCSE science courses and examinations will be such that students find them enjoyable and stimulating – that they can indeed do science, show that they can do it and understand the relevance of science in their lives.

REFERENCES

Assessment of Performance Unit (1985a) *Science at Age 15*, APU Science Report for Teachers 5, APU, London

Assessment of Performance Unit (1985b) *Practical Testing at Ages 11, 13 and 15*, APU Science Report for Teachers 6, APU, London

Association for Science Education (1985) The Common System of Examining at 16+, *Education in Science*, Vol. 113, pp. 11–12

Association for Science Education (in preparation) *Science and Technology in Society Project (SATIS)*, ASE, Hatfield

DES (1985a) *General Criteria, GCSE*, HMSO, London

DES (1985b) *The National Criteria, Science, GCSE*, HMSO, London

DES (1985c) *The National Criteria, Biology, GCSE*, HMSO, London

DES (1985d) *The National Criteria, Chemistry, GCSE*, HMSO, London

DES (1985e) *The National Criteria, Physics, GCSE*, HMSO, London

DES/Welsh Office (1985) *Science 5–16: A Statement of Policy*, HMSO, London

Graded Assessment in Science Project (1985) *Development Trials Package for Level One in Process Skills*. Inner London Education Authority/Chelsea College Centre for Science and Mathematics Education/University of London Examining Baord/London Regional Examining Board

Oxford Certificate of Educational Achievement (1985) *Pilot Phase: Teacher Guide – Science*, University of Oxford Delegacy of Local Examinations, Oxford

Chapter 10
GEOGRAPHY
Keith Orrell (*Leeds Polytechnic School of Education*)

> Geography is concerned to promote an understanding of the nature of the earth's surface and, more particularly, the character of places, the complex nature of people's relationships and interactions with their environment and the importance in human affairs of location and the spatial organisation of human activities.

This summary of the nature of geography is the opening paragraph of the *National Criteria for Geography* in the GCSE (SEC, 1985). Geographers are notoriously diverse in their views on the boundaries of their subject and this definition would satisfy few academics. However, it forms a useful starting point for considering the contribution the subject can make to the school curriculum. It certainly supports the view, 'First that some form of geography has an important place on the school curriculum and second that the curriculum must be able to respond rapidly to social, political and economic change in the real world' (Robinson, 1985).

The lay person seems to expect a geographical education to leave the pupil with an accumulation of world knowledge although this could equally be the outcome of a study of the history of India, or the literature of the United States. This acquisition of factual information about places has been a continuing, if declining, feature of school geography. The increasingly rapid pace of political, social, economic and even environmental change is quickly rendering information about places redundant. At the same time, the emphasis in schools on the learning experience has meant that styles of teaching and learning oriented towards recall are less and less attractive to pupils and teachers alike. However, it is worth noting that the National Criteria do require GCSE examinations to test the extent to which candidates are able to 'recall facts relating to the syllabus content and demonstrate locational knowledge within the range of small, regional, national, international and world scales' (SEC, 1985). The implication of this is not that there is an immutable body of information to be learned. However, there is a need for conceptual understanding and for 'an understanding of different communities and cultures within our own society and elsewhere in the world' (SEC, 1985, para. 2.1.5) to spring from an awareness of conditions in the real world – that is, from a sense of place.

The framework in which pupils in the past normally acquired world knowledge was a regionally based one. Natural or physical regions, often climatic at the continental scale (the monsoon lands), or geomorphological at the local scale (the South Downs), formed a convenient packaging of information for study term by term. It also allowed the exploration of the relationships between human occupance and the natural environment which provided a theoretical underpinning to classroom geography. However, explanation based on the opportunities and constraints provided by the natural environment has proved an unsatisfactory base for the analysis of patterns of human activity. This is especially so as technological advances have made possible the modification, control, and destruction of environments. While the people/environment theme is a continuing thread in school geography, it now takes much more account of the way people interact with their environments and have a role in modifying and creating them. Thus the *National Criteria for Geography* state that pupils should be able to:

> show an appreciation of the wide range of processes, including human actions, contributing to the development of:
> (i) physical, economic, social, political and cultural environments and their associated effects on the landscapes;
> (ii) spatial patterns and interactions which are important within such environments
> describe the interrelations between people's activities and the total environment and demonstrate an ability to seek explanations for them. (SEC 1985, paras. 3.3, 3.4)

Regional geography at its worst led to the accumulation of information about the main features, usually highly generalized, of a region and the use of regions to illustrate particular themes. Thus the Ganges valley was studied to illustrate the relationship of crop combinations with rainfall, while West Africa appeared on most syllabuses to exemplify the division of tropical lands into climatic zones, each producing export crops in demand in West European countries. Studies of this kind though having perhaps unwittingly promoted environmental determinism, took little account of cultural and political influences, and wholly ignored the reality of life for local people.

In its more enlightened form, regional geography, through sample studies and the lavish use of visual material and maps provided a more vivid and realistic image of different places. It established much good classroom practice which still serves the teacher, attempting to provide pupils with meaningful images, well. It is clearly impossible to present a comprehensive coverage of a very diverse world in this way. However the National Criteria do recognize the need for pupils to be aware of a representative range of environments. All courses should aim 'to develop an awareness of the characteristics and distribution of a selection of contrasting physical and human environments' (SEC, 1985, para. 2.1.2).

A fourth long-standing feature of school geography has been the spatial approach which has taken as its starting point the distribution in terrestrial space at a range of scales of a variety of phenomena. Until the 1960s, world maps of the distribution of precipitation, or wheat production, and maps of the United Kingdom showing the location of iron and steel production formed the basis of much classroom teaching and examining. Today, they are likely to have been replaced by maps of global inequalities in the quality of life, of contrasts in levels of unemployment between the standard regions of Britain, and of the access to medical services in an urban area. Spatial patterns form the starting point for much classroom investigation which leads to a greater understanding of the processes which influence environments, landscapes and ways of life. The National Criteria require all courses 'to promote an understanding of the spatial effects of the ways in which people interact with each other and with their environments'. All examinations will need to test the extent to which candidates are able to:

Show an appreciation of the wide range of processes, including human actions, contributing to the development of:
(i) physical, economic social political and cultural environments and their associated effects on landscapes;
(ii) spatial patterns and interactions which are important within such environments. (SEC, 1985, para. 3.3)

Thus, geography in the GCSE can be interpreted as retaining several long-standing characteristics of the subject in the classroom, albeit in a form more appropriate to the needs of young people growing up in the last two decades of the twentieth century. These are:
1 World knowledge and an awareness of what places are really like.
2 The identification and explanation of the interaction between people and environments.
3 The study of regions with contrasting physical and human environments.
4 The identification and explanation of spatial patterns.
Coupled with the imaginative use of visual aids, radio programmes, maps,

fieldwork and attractively produced textbooks, these starting points for geography teaching formed the basis for much excellent teaching in the early 1960s, a period which has been described as one of enlightened traditionalism (Beddis, 1983).

Much work in secondary schools, especially with 11–14-year-olds still follows this pattern and these traditional strands have been carried through into GCSE although in a modified form. What then is new about geography in GCSE?

In the mid-sixties the quantitative techniques being employed by university geographers began to attract the attention of teachers in schools. These statistical methods were linked to a more important movement – the search for order and recurring patterns in the landscape from which generalizations, theories and models could be generated. Thus the emphasis in geography swung away from the uniqueness of places towards what they had in common. For instance, the processes which influenced the pattern of market towns and villages in East Anglia could be seen to be the same as those responsible for settlement patterns in China. Generalizations and models are clearly useful in the geography classroom. They provide a yardstick against which to compare reality. They encapsulate concepts and ideas which can be exemplified and applied in many apparently different situations. The new scientific geography also encouraged a more overt development of skills, notably those linked to the testing and generation of hypotheses. In some ways however, the intellectual stimulus which the new geography gave teachers in the 1960s and early 1970s diverted attention from the more crucial curriculum issues. The *National Criteria for Geography* appear to give comparatively little prominence to quantitative techniques or model based approaches. However reference is made in para. 3.2 of the criteria to the ability to 'demonstrate a grasp of the geographical ideas, concepts, generalizations and principles specified in the syllabus and an ability to apply these to a variety of physical, economics, environmental, political and social contexts' (SEC, 1985). Also skills appropriate to geographical enquiries in which data collected both in the field and from secondary sources, analysis and interpretation are emphasized.

A new orthodoxy in which candidates would need to know the details of standard models of industrial location or urban structure has fortunately not replaced the old one in which information about classic regions like the Prairies had to be rote learned. However, what did emerge strongly from changes in the subject in the 1960s and 1970s was the adoption by schools of approaches based on concepts and key ideas well summarized by Her Majesty's Inspectorate in *The Teaching of Ideas in Geography* (HMI, 1978).

Most of the new GCSE syllabuses include concepts and key ideas as a major component of their content.

Throughout the 1970s geography teachers have tried to make the subject more relevant to the needs of their pupils. Consequently they have given increasing attention to the economic, environmental, social and political issues which arise naturally from a study of places and environments. A landmark in this respect was the publication by the Schools Council Geography for the Young School Leaver Project in 1974 and subsequently, its three packs of teaching materials entitled *Man, Land and Leisure, Cities and People*, and *People, Place and Work*.

These themes, a place to live, the world of work, and leisure have seen to contain important issues facing youngsters leaving school at sixteen and to provide springboards for studies at a variety of scales which geographical approaches could help them to appreciate and understand. Since then issues with a geographical dimension have been incorporated into many teaching programmes.

The National Criteria recognize the role of the subject in contributing to an understanding of issues by stating that:

> Geography is a valuable medium for education in a social context which includes such characteristics with a geographical dimension as:
> (a) a rapidly increasing world population with expanding consumer demand and consequent resource implications;
> (b) the existence of multicultural communities and societies;
> (c) the existence of marked contrasts in the level of economic and technological development between and within nations;
> (d) the occurrence of rapid social, economic and technological change in developed and developing countries;
> (e) an increase in environmental hazards and growing concern about the deteriorating quality of some environments. (SEC, 1985, para. 1.3)

Geographical understanding, and modes of enquiry, lend themselves well to a consideration of issues at a variety of scales ranging from local planning problems such as how to resolve a conflict of interests in utilizing a water storage reservoir for a variety of leisure activities, to questions concerned with national energy policies or population growth and food supplies at the global scale.

It is impossible to consider issues in the classroom without recognizing the importance of the values, attitudes, and perceptions of the groups and individuals involved. Decisions about the allocation of resources or the use of space can only be fully understood in terms of the goals and aspirations of those involved and especially of the decision makers. The National Criteria include references to values in both the aims and assessment objectives. Courses are required to encourage 'a sensitive awareness of the environment' and an 'awareness of the contrasting opportunities and constraints facing people living in different places under different physical and human conditions'. Candidates should also be required to use their geographical knowledge 'to demonstrate an awareness of the significance of attitudes and values in some current social, economic and environmental issues'. It would appear that courses and examinations are *not* required to encourage pupils to become aware of their own values and attitudes. Thus the emphasis is on values analysis rather than values clarification. Brian Maye has summarized the variety of approaches to values education as follows:

> *Values inculcation* has the objective that students will adopt a predetermined set of values.
>
> *Values analysis* uses structured discussion and logical analysis of evidence to investigate values issues.
>
> *Moral reasoning* provides opportunities to discuss reasons for value positions and choices with the aim of encouraging growth in moral reasoning ability.
>
> *Values clarification* has the objective of helping students become aware of their own values in relation to their behaviour and that of others.
>
> *Action learning* encourages students to see themselves as interacting members of social and environmental systems through having them analyse and clarify values with the intention of enabling them to act in relation to social and environmental issues according to their value choices. (Maye, 1984, p. 34)

Although Maye distinguishes here between values analysis, moral reasoning, and values clarification, they are clearly inseparable in a learning situation. Action learning stresses the teacher's role in encouraging students to see themselves as being part of, and actively involved in, social and environmental issues. The *National Criteria for Geography* do not seem to propose the wider view of values education recommended by Maye (1984). However, they do recognize that geography can 'provide a perspective in which they (the students) can place local, national and international events and enable them to function more effectively as individuals and members of society'. Values education within geography is clearly a new dimension to the subject given recognition, if in a limited way, within the National Criteria. The implications for the teacher are developed in the *GCSE Geographical Guide for Teachers* (SEC/OU, 1986) from which the following extract is taken:

In the past some teachers have avoided considering the role of values in geography in an attempt to appear neutral and non-doctrinaire. But in order to understand the character of places, and the behaviour of people in relation to their environments, we need to probe the motivations, values and emotions of the people involved. Maye draws attention to the fact that the decisions we make about what and how to teach are influenced by our own values and attitudes, for instance towards planning issues, environmental conservation and landscape quality.

Values education in geography is more than the development of an appreciation of the part played by the values and attitudes of people or groups in geographical situations, as the National Criteria emphasize in paragraph 3.7. It provides us with opportunities to assist students to develop their own self-concepts, emotions, values, decision and action skills in a geographical context. Maye suggests that when planning and implementing strategies for values teaching teachers should give careful consideration to the following points:

1 The teacher's own values will influence the topics and stimulus materials chosen and the way in which teaching strategies are implemented.
2 The teacher therefore needs to clarify his/her own values in relation to the topics chosen for study, and be clear in the purpose underlying the approach he/she chooses to follow. With very little change in emphasis and technique, a values analysis strategy could become (intentionally or unintentionally) a values inculcation strategy.
3 An atmosphere of mutual trust and respect in the classroom is necessary for values teaching to be successfully undertaken. Teacher sensitivity is essential.
4 Skilful questioning based on a clear sense of purpose is essential to promoting investigative skills in students.
5 Students should not be pressured into answering or participating in activities about which they are self-conscious. Permit them not to answer or participate if they so choose.
6 Students' responses will be inhibited by teacher moralising, criticism, evaluation of student values, or overt display of the teacher's values.
7 Evaluation of students' learning can be based on their ability to apply skills relating to valuing in practical activities and situations, rather than on values themselves (Maye, 1984, p. 42).

Mapwork forms the basis of many activities in the geography classroom. Indeed, map reading was the only clearly identifiable skills objective in most syllabuses at one time. Fieldwork was undertaken to illustrate classroom teaching at first hand and to provide an opportunity to use maps in a practical context. However the National Criteria reflect the extent to which skills have been given increasing emphasis in school geography in the last twenty years. They require courses 'to develop a range of skills' and examinations should test candidates' ability to 'select and use a variety of techniques appropriate to a geographical enquiry including investigation in the field'. Although maps, photographs and statistical data are given a specific mention, the emphasis is on the enquiry approach which calls on the more general skills of problem identification, selection and collection of data, analysis and interpretation; the evaluation of outcomes and the presentation of conclusions. This process of geographical enquiry has been defined more fully on many occasions, as for instance by the Schools Council Geography 16–19 Project (see Figure 10.1; also Hart, 1982).

While the need to develop enquiry skills are explicit, the criteria include more wide ranging implications for the development of general skills within the context of a geographical education. Courses are being asked to assist pupils to develop a sense of place, a sensitive awareness of the environment, an appreciation of the significance of the attitudes and values of decision-makers, and an awareness of the contrasting opportunities and constraints facing people living in different places, so that they can function more effectively as individuals and members of society. Slater (1982) suggests that 'it is at these growing edges that geography's role in developing political literacy and an ability to read, analyse clarify and interpret one's own and other people's values, interests and points of view coincides with some of the more general educational concerns for encouraging political understanding and educating affectively as well as cognitively'. The approach which brings together affective and cognitive learning – confluent education – is inherent in Figure 10.1 and has been well exemplified by Fien (1983) in diagrammatic form (see Figure 10.2). He points out that confluent education has as its goal a feeling-thinking person. This hopefully is the likely outcome of the kind of geography curriculum envisaged by the National Criteria. It remains to be seen whether or not the examining groups can generate syllabuses and examinations which foster it.

So far this discussion of geography in the GCSE has explored, first the form in which long-standing traditions have been retained; and second, the way in which some of the important changes which took place in the 1960s and 1970s in the teaching of the subject have been incorporated into the National Criteria. With this in mind, the key features of the criteria can be summarized. They are:

The need for factual knowledge to be acquired through the study of ideas and issues in real world settings at a variety of scales.

FACTUAL ENQUIRY	ROUTE AND KEY QUESTIONS	VALUES ENQUIRY
Achieve awareness of a question, issue or problem arising from the interaction of people with their environments.	**OBSERVATION AND PERCEPTION** *WHAT? and WHERE?*	Achieve awareness that individuals and groups hold differing values with regard to the question, issue or problem.
Outline and define the question, issue or problem. State hypothesis where appropriate. Decide on data and evidence to be collected. Collect and describe data and evidence.	**DEFINITION AND DESCRIPTION** *WHAT? and WHERE?*	List the values held or likely to be held by different individuals or groups with interest and/or involvement. Classify values into categories. Assess the actions likely to be linked with each category.
Organize and analyse data. Move towards providing answers and explanations. Attempt to accept or reject hypothesis. Decide whether more or different data and evidence are required.	**ANALYSIS AND EXPLANATION** *HOW? and WHY?*	Assess how far the values can be verified by evidence, i.e. to what extent are the values supported by facts? Produce ranked list of own preference or those of interested groups represented.
Evaluate results of enquiry. Attempt to make predictions, to move towards generalizations and theory construction. Consider future alternatives.	**EVALUATION, PREDICTION AND THEORY CONSTRUCTION** [WHAT WILL? and HOW OUGHT?]	Relate predictions and future alternatives to the preferred values.
Base decision on results of enquiry, and relate to results of values enquiry.	**DECISION-MAKING** *WHAT WILL? and HOW OUGHT?*	Base decision on results of enquiry, and relate to results of factual enquiry.

DECISION

Figure 10.2:   Confluent Education Applied to a Geographical Example (Fien, 1983)

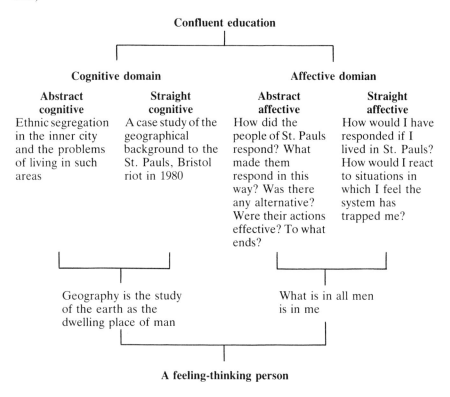

Confluent education

Cognitive domain   **Affective domian**

Abstract cognitive	**Straight cognitive**	**Abstract affective**	**Straight affective**
Ethnic segregation in the inner city and the problems of living in such areas	A case study of the geographical background to the St. Pauls, Bristol riot in 1980	How did the people of St. Pauls respond? What made them respond in this way? Was there any alternative? Were their actions effective? To what ends?	How would I have responded if I lived in St. Pauls? How would I react to situations in which I feel the system has trapped me?

Geography is the study of the earth as the dwelling place of man

What is in all men is in me

A feeling-thinking person

An emphasis on the relationships and interaction between people and environments and especially the process by which environments develop and change.

An understanding of ideas, concepts and generalizations and an ability to apply them in a variety of contexts.

The importance of studies of spatial patterns and processes.

The opportunity that geography provides to develop general as well as subject specific skills through geographical enquiries.

A recognition of the need both to understand the role of the values and attitudes of decision-makers involved in issues with a geographical dimension, and to help students to clarify their own values and attitudes.

A more recent and brisker statement of objectives for geography in secondary education has been provided by Trevor Bennetts, HMI Staff Inspector for Geography (1985). His ten objectives (see Figure 10.3)

Figure 10.3: Objectives for Geography in Secondary Education (11–16) (Bennetts, 1985)

The geographical component of the 11–16 curriculum should help pupils to:
1 further develop their understanding of their surroundings and extend their interest, knowledge and understanding of more distant places;
2 gain a perspective within which they can place local, national and international events;
3 learn about the variety of conditions on the earth's surface; the different ways in which people have reacted to, modified and shaped environments; and the influence of environmental conditions (physical and human) on social, political and economic activities;
4 appreciate more fully the significance in human affairs of the location of places and the links between places, and develop understanding of the spatial organisation of human activities;
5 gain understanding of the processes which have produced pattern and variety on the earth's surface and which bring about change;
6 develop a sensitive awareness of the contrasting opportunities and constraints facing different peoples living in different places under different economic, social, political and physical conditions;
7 develop an understanding of the nature of multicultural and multi-ethnic societies, a sensitivity to cultural prejudice, and values which reject racist views;
8 gain a fuller understanding of some important social, economic, political and environmental problems which have a geographical dimension, reflect on their own and other people's attitudes to these problems, and make their own informed judgements;
9 develop a wide range of skills and competencies that are required for geographical enquiry and are widely applicable in other contexts;
10 act more effectively in their environment as individuals and as members of society.

reiterate the key features of the National Criteria but are much more positive about the role of geography in values education. Some of the recently approved GCSE Geography syllabuses, notably those based on the Schools Council's Geography 14–18 (Bristol) Project and the Geography for the Young School Leaver (Avery Hill) project, also have clearer, more positive statements on values objectives.

When, a few years ago, the task of devising the National Criteria began, it was taking place in a changing curriculum environment in which doubts were already being expressed about the value of the new 'scientific' geography in schools. The *new*, new geographies – behavioural, welfare, humanistic and radical geographies – were beginning to be seen as having much to contribute to the students' education.

The *National Criteria for Geography* in the GCSE are in some ways then only a 'still frame' in the fast moving drama of curriculum change which has characterized geographical education over the last 25 years. In the view of Huckle (1983) recent curriculum reform has provided mechanisms for further change and current political and economic realities provide teachers with significant opportunities to exploit. School geography could begin to play a role in creating more fulfilled and happy individuals in a fairer, less troubled world (Huckle, 1983). The criteria rationalize, and make more widely available, many of the developments which have already been piloted by the Schools Council Geography Projects examinations and other 16+ schemes. They are also sufficiently flexible to permit teachers and examination groups to further develop imaginative yet relevant styles of teaching and assessment to meet the changing needs of pupils.

REFERENCES

Beddis, R. (1983) Geographical education since 1960: a personal view. In J. Huckle (1983) *Geographical Education*, Oxford University Press

Bennetts T. (1985) Geography from 5 to 16. A view from the Inspectorate. *Geography*, Vol. 70, Part 4, October

DES (1985) *General Certificate of Secondary Education: The National Criteria for Geography*, HMSO, London

Fien, J. (1983) Humanistic geography. In J. Huckle, (1983) *Geographical Education*, Oxford University Press

Hart, C. (1982) *Values Enquiry in Practice*. Occasional Paper No. 3, Schools Council Geography 16–19 Project, Longmans, York

HMI (1978) *The Teaching of Ideas in Geography*, HMSO, London

Huckle, J. (1983) The politics of school geography. In J. Huckle (1983) *Geographical Education*, Oxford University Press

Maye, B. (1984) Developing valuing and decision-making in the geography classroom. In J. Fein, R. Gerber and P. Wilson (1984) *The Geography Teachers' Guide to the Classroom*, Macmillan, Melbourne

Robinson, R. (1985) Ten years of change: influences on school geography 1972–1982. In D. Boardman (1985) *New Directions in Geographical Education*, Falmer Press, London

SEC (1985) *National Criteria for Geography*, SEC, London

SEC/Open University (1986) *GCSE Geography Guide for Teachers*, Open University Press, Milton Keynes

Slater, F. (1982) Literacy, numeracy and graphicacy in geographical education. In N. Graves *et al.* (1982) *Geography in Education Now*, Institute of Education, London University, London, pp. 18–27

Chapter 11
HISTORY
Paul Armitage (*Secondary Examination Council*) and Lawrence Taylor (*Berkshire County Council Adviser for Humanities*)

This paper seeks to explain the reasons behind and the nature of the major features of GCSE history and to demystify some aspects of this change. It also considers some possible ways forward as the new syllabuses become a reality in the classroom.

THE NATIONAL CRITERIA

What is perhaps the most dramatic change has occurred with the least comment – the implementation of an agreed set of National Criteria to which all history syllabuses and examinations need to conform. It is interesting to speculate on the reasons for this lack of comment. The most likely explanation is that the criteria reflect what has now become a consensus view on the nature of history as taught in British schools and what most teachers would accept as representing good practice. In this context, it is important to note that the major input to the criteria came from a broadly based group of teachers, advisers and others brought together for the purposes by the Joint Council of the GCE and CSE Boards. It is quite legitimate therefore to claim that the criteria are curriculum-led.

DIFFERENTIATION IN GCSE HISTORY

Differentiation raises many important issues for the historian – in particular how to devise appropriate assessment strategies which would genuinely encourage history students to show what they know, understand and can do.

As indicated elsewhere three principal strategies have been suggested for achieving differentiation: (1) differentiation papers, (2) stepping, and (3) differentiation by outcome. In GCSE history, however, the strategy which appears to be being favoured by historians is that of differentiation by outcome.

The reason for this is essentially very simple. Any attempt to differentiate by paper or by stepping implies that when constructing examination papers, examiners are certain they have identified a valid hierarchy of difficulty, i.e. that they know what is easy and what is difficult and that they have correctly targetted questions at appropriate levels in that hierarchy. In other words, examiners are certain that, for example, in a stepped question, those parts of the question targeted only at the more able are genuinely open only to the more able.

Now, in history such precision in targeting questions on precise levels of ability is probably impossible. For instance, if we think for a moment of a matrix of statements of different levels of candidate performance in course objectives, with skills on the horizontal axis and levels of performance in those skills on the vertical axis, such as is being developed in the grade criteria exercise, it will be appreciated that it would probably be very difficult for history examiners to target questions on any given level and indeed on any single individual skill.

In consequence, and in recognition of the difficulty, historians appear to be agreeing that differentiation must be by outcome whereby all questions are open to the full GCSE ability range and mark schemes are so constructed as to recognize different levels of positive achievement in candidates' responses.

Of course, differentiation by outcome raises many problems. For instance, it is no easy task to set questions which are open to the full ability range. It is equally difficult to create level mark schemes which recognize and reward positive achievement in the course objectives. Even when mark schemes have been created, examiners will have to remain vigilant to ensure that the schemes prove to be both correct and valid in terms of actual candidate-responses. Schemes such as that developed by the Southern Regional Examinations Board for the Schools Council History Project 13–16 CSE syllabus may become commonplace. The syllabus involves the pre-trialling of questions, a *post hoc* sampling of scripts with appropriate subsequent adjustment mark scheme and question weightings to conform to candidate-performance, and a longer-term post-mortem analysis (Wilmut, 1982; Hamer, 1982).

AIMS AND ASSESSMENT OBJECTIVES FOR HISTORY

The debate about aims and objectives in history has rumbled on since the publication of Coltham and Fines, *Educational Objectives for the Study of History* (1971). This pamphlet, based on the work on the American, Benjamin Bloom, set history teachers, inspectors and examiners along a new, and not always welcome, road. Pupils, teachers and examiners were urged to have a clear idea of what they were seeking to achieve in the teaching/learning process and of how they were to achieve it. In many respects the declaration of aims and assessment objectives in the National Criteria is the logical outcome of these earlier discussions. It also marks something of a victory for those who have urged that, rather than concentrating on content, much greater attention should be paid to defining what the important skills and concepts are so that pupils can be encouraged to develop them.

In general, teachers and examiners have welcomed this emphasis on objectives. For many, their inclusion in the GCSE represents nothing new. Certainly, many Schools History Project teachers are well versed in objectives-led teaching. Equally, SHP examiners are experienced in the careful construction of examination papers and mark schemes which ensure that selected objectives, or targets, are tested by the questions set.

However, other teachers and examiners are not so well versed in the new approach. Although objectives play a central role in the SHP, in other examinations their presence is almost cosmetic and mark schemes appear to recognize performance only in recalled facts. Certainly, there is evidence to suggest that in many examinations (even those where objectives are specified) it is recall that is consciously or unconsciously rewarded (Bradbury and Newbould, 1985; Orr and Forrest, 1984). For many teachers and examiners therefore (and it is probably safe to say that they are in the majority), the challenge of the GCSE will be considerable.

Although there is general support of objectives-led teaching, some qualifications have been raised of late (*TES*, 1985a; Duffy, 1985). Objectors tend to focus on the notion that 'history is more than this'. They reflect the view that breaking down the subject into isolated objectives undermines its nature and definition. They argue that it is often difficult, and in some respects impossible, to teach and examine to specific, isolated objectives. This is especially the case in humanities subjects where one is aiming at complex interrelationships of skills, concepts and knowledge and where the reduction of the 'art of history' into a few simple statements fails to do justice to the subject, students, teachers and examiners. Teachers and examiners are thus presented with virtually impossible tasks.

This is certainly a powerful view and has received considerable support from many quarters. However, at the same time there is a nagging fear that failure to support an objectives approach amounts to a form of intellectual laziness – an unwillingness to consider what one is really teaching and examining and how it should be taught and examined. Perhaps, therefore, the answer is not to regard objectives as sacred, but to take a more considered and pragmatic stance, fully aware of both their strengths and weaknesses.

Having made these general points, we now turn to comment on specific aims and objectives in the criteria. These are outlined in paragraphs 2 and 3 of the *National Criteria for History* (DES, 1985a). There are also what are effectively aims relevant to history in paragraph 19 of the General Criteria.

In general terms it is unlikely that many teachers or examiners will object to the aims and objectives. They are a basic and relatively uncontroversial set of statements and, as such, accurately mirror a contemporary and undogmatic view of what mainstream History is in the majority of British schools. The evidence-based approach is there (paras. 2.3 and 3.4); so too is the desire to locate, analyse and detect bias (paras 2.6 and 3.4). There is the declared aim (para. 2.2) of linking the past, where appropriate, to the present, and (para. 2.7) of actually providing students with the basis of a leisure-time pursuit. The aim (paras. 2.4 and 4.1) of helping 'pupils particularly in courses on British history, towards an understanding of the development over time of social and cultural values' (the subject of the so-called 'shared-values' debate), is open to different interpretations. Paragraphs 2.5 and 3.2 stress the need to understand key concepts which are widely accepted as crucial to history teaching and should leave most feathers unruffled. Paragraph 3.3, which deals with empathy, is a problem to the extent that empathy and the teaching thereof continues to raise important issues (Little, 1983).

More problematic for some history teachers and examiners is the set of aims contained in paragraph 19 of the General Criteria.

19(h) Avoidance of bias   Every possible effort must be made to ensure that syllabuses and examinations are free of political, ethnic, gender and other forms of bias.

19(i) Recognition of cultural diversity   In devising syllabuses and setting question papers, Examing Groups should bear in mind the linguistic and cultural diversity of society. The value to all candidates of incorporating material which reflects this diversity should be recognised.

19(j) Language   The language used in question papers (both rubrics and questions) must be clear, precise and intelligible to candidates throughout the range of entry for the examination. Examining Groups should consider whether they need to make special provision for candidates whose mother tongue is not English.

19(k) Emphases to be encouraged in all subjects   All syllabuses should be assessed as well as, or better, in course work than formal, written examinations. Indeed some skills and abilities (e.g. oral work) cannot be assessed in any other way.

It does, however, raise considerable problems, not least for those teachers who are not used to the formal assessment of coursework for examination purposes. For these teachers (and this applies particularly to teachers who have formerly been concerned only with GCE), the introduction of coursework presents a challenge. It also creates a vast moderation problem for examiners, not least to ensure comparability in assessing coursework in all the many centres. It could also easily create the further problem of seriously over-burdening both teachers and students because coursework is now a feature of all GCSE subjects.

The history criteria say very little about coursework apart from stating that normally a minimum of 20 per cent of marks should be derived from it. Nowhere is there any mention of the form that course work should take.

The SEC/Open University guide for history teachers is quite adventurous on this point. It expresses forcefully the hope that teachers and examiners will look beyond traditional types of coursework (invariably the 'project') to consider alternative forms of coursework including 'continuous' or 'periodic' assessment. The adoption of these would enable more, or possibly all, of the normal everyday classroom and homework activities to be taken into account for assessment purposes. It would also be a chance to introduce profiling/records of achievement (Armitage and Taylor, 1986).

The view taken in the guide is that although projects often work well (and therefore have a legitimate place in the GCSE), other forms of coursework would be more flexible and could be adjusted more readily to suit the needs of individual candidates. Differentiation in coursework could thus be more readily achieved and so too could 'fitness for purpose' (defined by paragraph 33 of the General Criteria as the development of examination components and assessment procedures which reflect and are appropriate to 'the nature of the subject, its educational aims and its assessment objectives'). Finally, the guide suggests that a more regular assessment of everyday activities could help to reduce over-burdening candidates and teachers.

There are then considerable possibilities within GCSE for coursework. It remains to be seen how many will be realized. Certainly there appear to be strong pressures to retain the present 'project' approach, in part because this is the form of coursework with which teachers and examiners are most familiar. Indeed, this familiarity may well ensure that projects do successfully differentiate and are 'fit for purpose'. Nevertheless, it is to be hoped that teachers and examiners will be prepared to explore new ground most suited to candidate needs.

CONCLUSION

Two further points remain. First, it will no longer be possible to pretend that the examination at 16+ is something divorced from the 5–14 or 16–18 curriculum. A good deal of harmonization will be needed to ensure that pupils learn the skills, content and concepts of history progressively throughout the years of schooling. This implies the need from the start for a much clearer statement of aims and objectives in history and much greater concern for continuity – particularly at the transition from one phase of schooling to the other. The publication of pamphlets such as *The Curriculum from 5 to 16* (DES, 1985c) and LEA curriculum guidelines in history and humanities has indicated the scale of the problem which has now to be tackled. But the implication of the GCSE for history does not end here. The survival of history in a world which has grown less sympathetic to its claims, however well founded and argued, will depend not only on the quality of the experience offered but also on the manner in which the subject is presented to its potential audience. The past, whether remote or near-contemporaneous offers tremendous riches of people, events, themes and varieties of evidence. It also provides a wide range of perspectives for looking at ourselves and the society in which we live. Unless we learn how to use the many possibilities history offers as a tool for understanding ourselves and our predicaments (perhaps in association with other subjects such as economics and politics) the subject, despite its present popularity, could disappear. In many ways the GCSE may well provide us with the breathing space necessary to look again at history and its image and to rejuvenate it for coexistence in a world where concern with values aligned to the market place has to be recognized.

REFERENCES

Armitage P. and Taylor L. (1986) *History GCSE: A Guide for Teachers*, Open University Press, Milton Keynes

Bradbury, R. and Newbould, C. (1985) *Knowledge and Analysis in History*, UCLES, Cambridge

Coltham, J. B. and Fines J. (1971) *Educational Objectives for the Study of History: A Framework*, Historical Association, London

Department of Education and Science (1985a) *The National Criteria, History*, HMSO, London

Department of Education and Science (1985b) *History in the Primary and Secondary Years: HMI View*, HMSO, London

Department of Education and Science (1985c) *The Curriculum from 5 to 16*, HMSO, London

GCSE AND THE SCHOOLS

Chapter 12
PREPARING TEACHERS FOR THE GCSE
Bill Prescott (*Open University*)

There is to my knowledge, no precedent for a programme of quite this kind, designed as it will be to provide help and support for such a large number of teachers over a relatively short period. (Sir Keith Joseph, 21 December 1984)

Sir Keith Joseph's letter to Sir Wilfred Cockcroft confirmed that the Department of Education and Science were fully aware that the GCSE in-service training programme, which they were initiating, had no precedent within England and Wales. On what assumptions, then, was this programme based? And what did the DES hope it would achieve?

The DES view on the in-service programme is contained in the letter of 21 December quoted above. Here it is suggested that the in-service should be organized in three phases in the form of a 'cascade' model.

Phase 1 (January to December 1985). Examining Groups would appoint subject experts who would first join the Secondary Examinations Council in the collective preparation of guides and videos which would be common to all Examining Groups and available to all GCSE teachers, and then organize the Phase 2 seminars in consultation with the LEAs, schools and colleges.

Phase 2 (January to July 1986). Experts from the Examining Groups would provide 2–2½ day seminars for an estimated 60 000 subject representatives as well as LEA experts and teacher trainers.

Phase 3 (January 1986 onwards). LEAs, schools and colleges would arrange for subject representatives and LEA experts to give similar seminars and briefings for the estimated remaining 126 000 GCSE teachers, preferably by September 1986, and provide the 'necessary follow-through subsequently especially in relation to setting and assessing actual GCSE coursework assignments'.

The same letter also indicated the pattern of responsibilities envisaged by the DES:

(a)   *Examining Groups* should be responsible for setting out the stan-
        dards and techniques of assessment required; for providing the Phase
        2 briefings; and for ensuring (in collaboration with the LEAs) that all
        GCSE teachers who would be assessing coursework would have
        received appropriate briefings.
(b)   *Schools and colleges* would be responsible for nominating subject
        representatives to attend Phase 2 seminars.
(c)   *LEAs* should be responsible for ensuring that all teachers received
        the necessary briefings; for organizing and contributing to briefings
        at a local level wherever appropriate.
(d)   The *SEC* should be responsible (in collaboration with the Examining
        Groups) for the preparation and dissemination of the GCSE
        teachers' guides and videos, and for administering the government's
        financial contribution.

This financial contribution would take the form of £6 million available for
the replacement of teachers attending the Phase 2 seminars (subsequently
increased to £8 million and extended to Phase 3 in-service work), and rather
less than £1 million to the SEC and Examining Groups to pay for the guides
and videos and to contribute towards the costs of employing subject experts.

The letter of 21 December appeared only five weeks after the DES had
distributed its 'provisional ideas' on how the in-service training should be
organized. Roger Murphy noted that:

> Even by current DES standards the time allowed for discussing the
> proposals was somewhat truncated, and it could hardly be said that a wide
> range of interested parties was consulted. . . . Needless to say, the
> announcement in December bore a close resemblance, in every detail, to
> the November proposals. (Murphy, 1985)

Although the two documents were clearly very similar, there were some
differences which are perhaps worth identifying in an attempt to explore the
assumptions on which the DES was working. Four points of difference are
perhaps worth noting:

1   The emphasis on training

The November draft proposals constantly use the term 'training'. The
cascade model was presented in its purest form: the Examining Groups
would appoint experts with overall responsibility for training; these experts
would train the heads of department; the heads of department would train
the teachers in their departments. However, in the December letter this
emphasis on training had all but disappeared. Instead, the Examining

Group will be responsible for providing 'briefings' and 'seminars'. Was this a sudden conversion to a more professional view of teachers – sharing experience among equals in a seminar, rather than being fodder for trainers? Or was it a reluctant acceptance that all that could be done was to ensure that opportunities for training were provided – and trust that teachers would attend?

2   The role of the Examining Groups

The draft proposals offered a quasi-mystical view of the Examining Groups as the 'repositories of wisdom and experience' in the field of assessment, bearing the 'primary responsibility for standards of training'. In the December letter, the language was somewhat different; the groups playing a 'key role in the programme of preparatory briefings' but now with an emphasis on collaboration – particularly with the LEAs. Had the period of consultation brought the DES to a realization that the Examining Groups had had a very limited role in INSET, while the LEAs have clearly been the major providers?

3   The role of heads of department

The November draft proposals envisaged a strong middle-management role for heads of department, who were to have 'new and special responsibilities for training their own staff and for confirming to the Examining Groups that these staff had been trained'. The DES hoped that 'there would be general agreement that it would be valuable, appropriate and effective to extend the responsibilities of heads of departments in this way'. It was even suggested that there might be 'a case for formal accreditation of trained teachers'. However, very little remained of this bold excursion in the December letter. The confident identification of heads of department was replaced by reference to 'subject representatives' and no reference whatsoever was made to any 'new and special responsibilities'.

4   The role of the DES

Under the draft proposals the DES would propose how the training programme should be organized, help secure agreement between all those concerned, and provide financial support.

   The December letter removed all reference to the DES in listing the responsibilities of the different participants. The commitment to providing financial support was elaborated in the letter but there was no reference to the organization of the training programme. The implication appeared to be that this had been achieved by the five weeks of consultation and the letter represent the limit of the DES's initiative in this respect. The responsibility for further contact was placed with the SEC or the Examining Groups: 'We stand ready to help in any way we can.'

What implications can be drawn from the changes between these documents? In the earlier proposals the DES was clearly taking a starkly 'agricultural' approach to innovation. The agricultural expert, having proved the superiority of the new variety of seed, carries the message to the agricultural extension workers, who in turn train the farmers. What could be more straightforward? After all, no one doubts the superiority of the seed; it is simply a question of disseminating the message. In the December letter, the model was somewhat fudged. The language was less confident, the lines of responsibility less clearly identified. However in important respects the model remained the same, and the DES was still able to determine the nature of the operation through its control of the timetable and the funding.

One of the intriguing aspects of this initiative was that although the DES recognized that the in-service programme was unprecedented, it nowhere explained the grounds for its commitment to the cascade approach. The clear implication was that, given the timetable imposed on the educational world, it was impossible to conceive of any other approach to training which could succeed. However there was no reference to any other country or comparable area of training where this approach had been successful.

SCOTTISH EXPERIENCE

One country which the DES might have referred to was Scotland. In Lanark attempts at a centre-periphery model to promote change in assessment policy and practice had been tried, and the experience charted by Black and colleagues between the years 1980 and 1983 (Black, 1985). The Lanark initiative differed in two important respects from the DES model for the GCSE. First, the Lanark approach was concerned with whole school policies and not simply with a subject approach to assessment. In this respect it might be argued that the Lanark task was more formidable (although possibly ultimately more worthwhile?). Second, the Lanark approach assumed the need for much more extensive training sessions than did the DES cascade model. Figure 12.1, from Black, indicates just how much in-service was involved. It should be compared with the DES strategy which had concluded that it would not be practicable for the briefings to exceed 2 or $2\frac{1}{2}$ days.

Figure 12.1: Dissemination Strategy within the Initiative

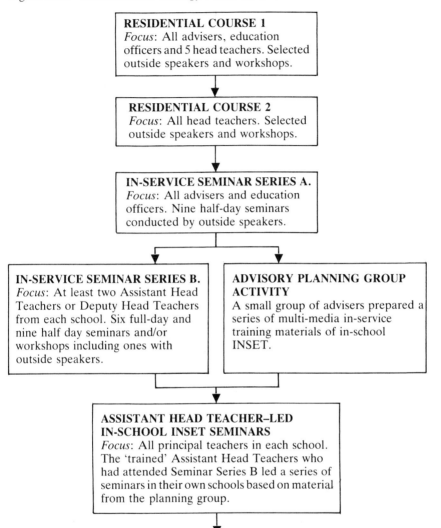

RESIDENTIAL COURSE 1
Focus: All advisers, education officers and 5 head teachers. Selected outside speakers and workshops.

RESIDENTIAL COURSE 2
Focus: All head teachers. Selected outside speakers and workshops.

IN-SERVICE SEMINAR SERIES A.
Focus: All advisers and education officers. Nine half-day seminars conducted by outside speakers.

IN-SERVICE SEMINAR SERIES B.
Focus: At least two Assistant Head Teachers or Deputy Head Teachers from each school. Six full-day and nine half day seminars and/or workshops including ones with outside speakers.

ADVISORY PLANNING GROUP ACTIVITY
A small group of advisers prepared a series of multi-media in-service training materials of in-school INSET.

ASSISTANT HEAD TEACHER–LED IN-SCHOOL INSET SEMINARS
Focus: All principal teachers in each school. The 'trained' Assistant Head Teachers who had attended Seminar Series B led a series of seminars in their own schools based on material from the planning group.

SUBJECT DEPARTMENT DISSEMINATION
Focus: All school staff below Principal Teachers level. Principal teachers now disseminated the content of Assistant Head Teacher-led seminars to staff in their departments.

What lessons might the Lanark experience have had for the GCSE in-service exercise?

First, although teachers broadly speaking approved the changes which were being introduced, this offered no guarantee that they would respond positively to the chosen method of communicating these changes. The DES, in insisting on the timetable set out in the December letter, presumably believed that an education profession united in support of GCSE, would not wish to prejudice its introduction. The Lanark experience indicated that this argument may cut little ice at the grass-roots level. This, indeed, was the argument put forward by the headteachers in support of a delay in the introduction of the GCSE.

Second, in a centre-periphery model much depends upon the commitment and skills of the disseminators – in Lanark, the assistant heads and principal teachers; in the cascade model the group experts and the subject representatives. If these 'middle managers' express doubts about the changes the model becomes far less plausible as an agent of change. Moreover even where there is commitment, there is not necessarily skill: heads of department may not necessarily possess in-service training skills. Black noted that:

> The comment of many disseminators suggested that they felt ill-trained for their endeavour and it may well be that those managing similar such exercises would be well-advised to look into strategies for training the trainers how to train. (Black, 1985)

The DES statements on the cascade model have little or nothing to say about the training skills of the subject representatives. The implication in the documents is that the Phase 3 training will be very much like the Phase 2 seminars, and that the subject representatives will 'give similar seminars and briefings for all other GCSE teachers'. The notes prepared for the group experts by the Open University and the SEC, and the supporting materials prepared by some of the groups were designed at least in part to emphasize the importance of in-service skills for Phase 3. But it was asking a great deal of the Phase 2 sessions that they should introduce subject representatives to the new features of the GCSE and impart in-service training skills – all within two days!

Third, in a centre-periphery model of innovation teachers should not feel that most of the resources have been provided for the centralized activity and relatively little for the schools. Unfortunately this appeared to be the case in the cascade model. The DES funded the preparation of the training materials and a proportion of the costs involved in replacing heads of department, but originally planned to provide nothing for Phase 3. The provision of the guides to all GCSE teachers at the beginning of the exercise was a clear improvement on the Scottish arrangements, where the assistant teachers felt they were left in the dark until it came to their turn to be involved. However the DES showed no sympathy for the Scottish expedient of closing the schools for 5–10 days in term time to assist school-based training.

Later the policy was somewhat revised. Due to underspending on the in-service budget the DES was able to 'find' £2 million extra for Phase 3 to provide cover for teachers attending seminars for which the rate of grant was increased from 70 per cent to 90 per cent.

The Scottish experience, as exemplified by the Lanark initiative, was not therefore an altogether encouraging precedent for the cascade model – particularly since there was little to suggest that the DES had anticipated the problems identified by Black.

INTENDED OUTCOMES OF THE CASCADE PROGRAMME

What did the DES see as a successful outcome of the in-service programme? The DES considered that teachers needed to be familiar with three innovations in the new system: the National Criteria, assessment objectives (particularly the complexities of differentiation), and coursework assessment.

With respect to coursework the DES emphasized that they would like to see as much consistency and comparability as possible across the country between internal assessment techniques. Indeed this argument was used to support the production of the national guides and videos which were prepared by the Open University on behalf of the Secondary Examinations Council.

Given the subject orientation of the GCSE, the three targets set by the DES do not seem unreasonable. However two kinds of tension were predictable in the programme. First, should the in-service work focus on a relatively straightforward implementation of the changes – or should it allow for debate and criticism? For example, the National Criteria for home economics were, in parts, virtually impenetrable and, arguably, should never have been approved in their present form. Should teachers, nevertheless, be told that they must take these criteria as given? How much time should be devoted to encouraging them to come forward with modifications? This issue had already had to be faced in the writing of the guides, and the policy adopted had been, by and large, to side-step such problems and concentrate on the positive aspects of the new examination. The result has been that awkward issues which may vex teachers have occasionally been avoided, and not surprisingly this had meant a blander guide than would have resulted from a more robust approach. The difference here, however, is that the writing of a guide can be controlled in this way; it is far more difficult to so control an in-service seminar – yet alone a school-based session.

Second, the DES envisaged Phases 1 and 2 and perhaps Phase 3 as being concerned with general principles and not with any specific syllabus prepared by an Examining Group. In theory, schools and colleges would subsequently choose from the various syllabuses on the basis of an informed judgement about the appropriateness of different approaches for their particular situation. However the timetable imposed on the exercise made this problematic. For at the point when many teachers were attending Phase 2 seminars, and certainly by the time schools had begun Phase 3, decisions had to be made about the particular syllabuses that were to be followed. It was probably too much to expect that the Examining Groups which were organizing the Phase 2 sessions would introduce participants to a range of approaches adopted by different groups. The most that could be expected was illustrated by this extract from the Midland Examining Group newsletter:

> The overall aim is to provide generalised subject training. However, where examples are used to develop a teaching point, they will normally be taken from an appropriate MEG syllabus. (MEG, 1985)

But what about the consistency and comparability which the DES hoped would result from the in-service exercise? Given this expressed wish, it may be thought curious that the DES has exercised no coordinating role over the programme. As was mentioned earlier, it has controlled the timing and the funding but has declined to offer any leadership or coordination. What coordination there has been has come through the Advisory Committee set up by the SEC. However it could be argued that a greater measure of concern for the implementation of the programme might have resulted in a greater dissemination of good ideas and initiatives. For example the Midland Examining Group introduced what it called a Phase $1\frac{1}{2}$ for headteachers and LEA advisers which was specifically designed to rectify a clear gap left in the DES cascade strategy. The lack of attention paid to such staff should be compared with the approach adopted in the Lanark initiative described earlier. The same group also negotiated with its LEAs the full-time secondment of a number of teachers to help with Phase 1 and Phase 2. Were these initiatives considered and rejected by the other groups? It is not immediately obvious why the records-of-achievement initiative required a national steering committee but the 'unprecedented' GCSE in-service programme did not. In addition it should be remembered that the groups are to a large extent competing against each other for customers. In such a free-market economy there is no reason why they should go out of their way to help their competitors – except perhaps that it might help towards the general objective identified by Sir Keith Joseph: 'to give teachers all the help and support we can in order that the new examination may be as good as possible'.

ALTERNATIVE APPROACHES

Finally, having raised a number of problems with the DES cascade model, it seems reasonable to ask what might an alternative model for this 'unprecedented programme' have looked like? Let us start with some alternative assumptions from those suggested in the DES documents:

1   The GCSE and the national criteria are not simply about changes in examination practice; they are designed to influence strongly if not actually determine the curriculum in secondary schools.
2   A strategy for effective curriculum change needs to begin with a consideration of the present position of schools and their perceived needs.
3   A school-focused approach to change does not rule out a role for external agencies; indeed the local authority support staff in particular should play a more crucial role than was anticipated in the cascade model.
4   The introduction of National Criteria makes it all the more important for Mode 3 examinations to be readily available; this implies that schools should have time to review existing syllabuses and prepare alternatives.

How might these assumptions have been translated into a strategy? A possible model might have looked something like this:

Phase 1. The national criteria are distributed to schools, Examining Groups, etc. The SEC/SCDC (in collaboration) invite the Open University to prepare in-service packs on the subjects covered by the national criteria and on the school-wide implications.

Phase 2. Schools (supported by local authority staff) and Examining Groups consider the issues of differentiation, coursework, planning school assessment policy, etc. with the help of the centrally produced materials.

Phase 3. Examining Groups prepare syllabuses for approval by the SEC.

Phase 4. Schools consider the appropriateness of the syllabuses in the light of their curriculum objectives, preparing Mode 3 syllabuses where necessary.

Phase 5. Schools receive briefing and training by relevant Examining Groups.

Such a strategy would acknowledge that since the GCSE is intended to help to improve practice and be much more than GCE and CSE under another name, the time-scale needs to be more realistic. Sir Keith Joseph told Parliament in 1984: 'I am surprised that those concerned tell me that we shall be able to introduce the new courses two years from now. It is rather sooner than I had expected when I proposed the policy in general at Sheffield earlier this year' (Hansard, 20 June 1984). Who were 'those concerned'? Sadly Hansard does not record whether there were cries of 'Name one!'

REFERENCES

Black, H. D. (1985) Centre-peripheral change in assessment – does it work? Paper presented at BERA Conference, Sheffield
Midlands Examining Group (1985) *GCSE In-Service Training Newsletter 1*, October
Murphy, Roger (1985) Innovation without change, *Times Educational Supplement*, 8 February

Chapter 13
TEACHING TO THE EXAM? THE CASE OF
THE SCHOOLS COUNCIL HISTORY PROJECT
John Scarth (*Open University*)

INTRODUCTION

A common system of examining at 16+ was long considered necessary to overcome the divisiveness and inefficiency of two separate systems. However the proposals to introduce the GCSE met with widespread criticism (Bowe and Whitty, 1983; Nuttall, 1984; Macintosh, 1985; Torrance, 1985). At the heart of this critical commentary was a concern that the DES, through the national criteria specifying the requirements for subject syllabuses, would increase its control over the education system. Macintosh claimed that the introduction of the GCSE reflected:

> growing central control in the process, practices and content of education and a realization by government that public examinations provide the most effective and final control. (Macintosh, 1985, p. 7)

Nuttall also noted that the GCSE would give the DES a marked increase in control over the secondary school curriculum:

> The DES have taken upon themselves a much more overt role in steering examination reforms and giving themselves rights (unprecedented since 1945) over the approval of the detailed content of examination syllabuses and schemes of examination since it is the DES that has the final say over the national criteria. Having failed in their attempts to control or influence markedly the curriculum through documents like *A Framework for the School Curriculum*, they can succeed by another route. (Nuttall, 1984, p. 174)

Nuttall argued that the control the DES would gain over the curriculum would have three main effects. First, the national criteria would regulate the number of subjects and syllabuses available and would consequently reduce the range of choice open to teachers. The 'professional autonomy' of teachers to design a curriculum to suit the pupils in their school would similarly be reduced. Second, with the replacement of the Schools Council by the Secondary Examinations Council, its membership nominated by the Secretary of State, teacher influence on national examinations policy would be reduced and hence decision-making would be still further concentrated at the centre. Third, the autonomy of the Examination Boards would be reduced. This, Nuttall feared, would further 'curb the autonomy of the teachers in their schools and classrooms' (Nuttall, 1984, p. 174).

Both Macintosh and Nuttall, then, thought that the GCSE would not only limit what teachers teach but also restrict how they teach in the classroom. Now that we have a better idea of what the new system is like are these fears proving justified?

With regard to DES control over what the teacher teaches, it does seem likely that there will be less choice for the teacher (Bowe and Whitty, 1983; Macintosh, 1985). Even though the GCSE incorporates some of the more progressive developments that have emerged out of Mode 3 examining, the potential for further development seems likely to be severely limited (Torrance, 1985). Much less attention has been given to the other main concern: that GCSE examinations may also limit how teachers teach. Here the issue of control seems much more complex. On the face of it, GCSE examinations appear to increase control over this dimension of teaching, too. For example history courses now include a local history component which may require teachers to adopt a new and different teaching style (e.g. leaving the classroom and going into the locality). However, teachers may also decide that their existing teaching methods are adequate and appropriate for the teaching of local history. In this case, new course content is approached as any other part of the course and is taught in much the same way. Central control over subject content does not necessarily mean loss of teachers autonomy over how subject material is taught any more than absence of central control indicates the existence of teacher autonomy.

Control over teaching, then, should not be conceived simply in terms of 'central control' and 'teacher autonomy'. Control over teachers' classroom practice takes many forms, from national policies through regional Examination Board regulations, to a great many 'local' factors (school ethos, resources, teacher biography, pupil subculture, etc.). Because of this the net effect on teachers of both national criteria and differentiated assessment may be less profound than many would expect. One reason for this is that very often the apparent failure to implement curriculum innovations successfully is a result of planners' unawareness of the routine nature of teachers' classroom practices (Bossert, 1979; Fullan, 1981), or to put it more bluntly, a failure to see the changes implied by the innovation from the teachers' point of view. As a result teachers are able to accommodate the implementation into their established patterns of work. The changes in assessment practices under GCSE may also be similarly absorbed into teachers' existing styles of teaching.

The influence of examinations on teaching was the specific focus of a recent research investigation, in which teaching on a number of different assessed and non-assessed courses was studied in detail (Hammersley and Scarth, 1986). Part of this work involved looking at the implementation of the Schools Council 13–16 History Project (SCP). While SCP under GCE and CSE regulations may not capture the full flavour of the GCSE history syllabus, nevertheless much is common between the two. For example, in an address delivered to the Historical Association's conference in 1984, the Secretary of State for Education, Sir Keith Joseph, emphasized that the national criteria for history should not be concerned with a traditional emphasis on factual recall:

> One of the consequences of a clearer view of objectives will, I hope, be the elimination of what I call clutter. By this I do not mean the removal of whole subjects. History [. . .] is not clutter. What I would like to see removed are certain aspects of teaching history. Do we, for example, sometimes place too much emphasis on the accumulation of unrelated facts? (Joseph, 1984, p. 32)

And he made it clear that, in his view, history should be concerned with the development of skills:

> History teaching can [. . .] encourage young people to use their reason as well as their memories. It can develop skills of analysis and criticism in a situation in which there cannot be a provably right answer, by encouraging pupils to evaluate primary source material. (Joseph, 1984, p. 32)

The SCP matched such concerns very closely. Given this, and the influence it seems to have had on the GCSE history criteria, it may be useful to examine the teaching of this course as a basis for assessing the likely effects of the GCSE.

THE SCHOOLS COUNCIL HISTORY 13–16 PROJECT: PHILOSOPHY AND ASSESSMENT

The SCP was established in 1972 and introduced to trial schools in 1973. The numbers of candidates entered for the course then increased rapidly each year. In 1976 there were 1228 candidates (less than 1 per cent of all history

O-level candidates); by 1984 this figure had increased to 18 014 (approximately 15 per cent of all history O-level candidates).

The origins of the project lay in two quite different but related sources. The project was a response to opportunities offered by the new history movement (Ballard, 1970; Rogers, 1978). It was also set up to meet the perceived challenge to the place of history in the school curriculum from the growth of integrated and social science subjects (Price, 1968; Shemilt, 1980; Brown and Daniels, 1983). The shape and nature of the project were largely determined by the terms of reference laid down by the history subject committee of the Schools Council:

(a) to examine the role of history in an era of curriculum change;
(b) to revitalize history teaching by giving institutional support;
(c) to encourage pupil participation in learning;
(d) to investigate ways of assessing understanding rather than rote-learning in public examinations. (Shemilt, 1980, p. 1)

The project team sought to justify the subject in terms of adolescent needs rather than simply seeing it as a scholarly pursuit, valid in its own right, or as preparation for more advanced studies. They identified five ways in which history was necessary and useful for adolescents to study:

1 The need to understand the world in which they live.
2 The need to find their personal identity by widening their experience through the study of people of a different time and place.
3 The need to understand change and continuity in human affairs.
4 The need to begin to acquire leisure interests.
5 The need to develop the ability to think critically, and to make judgements about human situations. (Schools Council, 1976, p. 12)

The project team also questioned the sort of historical knowledge which should be taught in schools. For them, the crucial component was not chronology but the nature of historical enquiry itself:

At the secondary level, this involves, first, introducing pupils to the historian's methods, asking 'How do we know?', evaluating evidence and using it to establish 'facts' and arbitrate amongst competing 'explanations'. Second, it involves adolescents learning something of the logic of history and the meaning of such key ideas as 'change', 'development', 'cause and effect' and so on; finally, it involves introducing pupils to some of the various approaches to history – the line of development, the depth study, contemporary history and local history. (Shemilt, 1980, p. 4)

Assessment was by two written examination papers and coursework. The examination accounted for 60 per cent of the final assessment and the remaining 40 per cent was allocated to coursework assessment (GCE and CSE requirements were the same).

Teachers devised assignments, weighted them within this framework, marked them and then sent the marks for all their candidates to the Examining Board. A sample was then selected by the Board for moderation purposes and the school was informed about changes to the marks awarded.

One indication of the nature of the control of assessment over teachers is the speed with which teachers comply with new assessment regulations. In the SCP there appears to have been some distance at first between the project team's ideals and the coursework produced:

> Copious copying from local guidebooks, mechanical recording in their diaries, without personal comment, and the lack of any spark or sparkle in other parts of their course work conveyed the impression of industrious pupils who were intent upon browbeating both their teacher and the examiner with the very volume of their encyclopaedic knowledge. Dictated notes and reams of duplicated plans, maps and detailed questionnaires increased the weight of the course work. (Chief Examiner's Report, Southern Universities Joint Board, summer 1977)

However, there is evidence that by 1983 schools had in fact made some adjustments and were now producing coursework closer to the project aims:

> This year 62% of centres had their marks left unchanged. It is tempting to conclude that this increase of 10% over last year reflects a growing awareness of appropriate ways to meet the requirements of coursework. (Chief Examiner's Report, Southern Universities Joint Board, summer 1983)

The written examinations were designed to assess knowledge of both course material and acquired skills. Paper 1 was more explicitly concerned with testing knowledge of course content. Paper 2 was a test of historical skills: a number of extracts from different sources relating to the same event (which was not part of the course content) were presented to candidates, who then had to interpret these sources in order to answer the questions. Often there was no 'right' or 'wrong' answer; the emphasis was on the candidate's reasoning and use of evidence. Both Paper 1 and Paper 2 were given the same weighting, each carrying 30 per cent of the final assessment.

The first three examinations (1976, 1977 and 1978) were used to pilot questions. Subsequent analysis of the examination questions, the evaluation report and the marking of the examination papers showed that questions on Paper 1 had been much less successful in matching project aims than questions on Paper 2. This 'failure' of Paper 1 in 1976, 1977 and 1978 was the result, Macintosh (Secretary, Southern Regional Examination Board) claims, of questions demanding detailed knowledge of specific content. Macintosh argues that the reason for this was simple:

> Paper 1 was the only part of the whole assessment which formally covered the Project's syllabus and as such it was felt that candidates ought to be able to demonstrate their knowledge of its content in some depth. Unfortunately, this was assessed as an end in itself and not as a vehicle through which candidates could demonstrate their mastery of the Project's aims. (Macintosh, 1979, p. 23)

This last remark is significant for it indicates that the aim behind the SCP was not so much that pupils should have a detailed knowledge of sections of the course, but that they should be able to demonstrate mastery of historical analysis. Questions designed to test this view would necessarily be of a different type to those simply requiring recall of information (see Macintosh, 1979, p. 24).

In both papers, then, the emphasis was on testing acquired skills rather than memory, a point stressed by the O-level Chief Examiner in several reports:

> More disturbing still was the growing habit of memorising a list of factors which inhibited change and then applying them to any historical problem regardless of the context of the period. (Chief Examiner's Report, Southern Universities Joint Board, summer 1982)

> In evaluating the response of candidates to this paper examiners were more concerned to discover and reward quality of thought rather than to weigh the answer on a quantitative basis. Brief answers which revealed a high level of conceptual ability, an understanding of historical skills and a capacity to see beyond the obvious were generously rewarded. (Chief Examiner's Report, Southern Universities Joint Board, summer 1980)

Moreover, the Chief Examiner was quite explicit that traditional examination techniques, for example carefully preparing answers in readiness for 'spotted' questions, were inappropriate to teaching on the SCP:

> The most worrying feature of this [using prepared answers] was the role of the teacher in certain centres. The similarity of the essays provided within these centres strongly suggested that the candidates entered the examination with carefully rehearsed essays in readiness for spotted questions. This practice placed the candidates at a considerable disadvantage, partly because, if the topic did occur they failed to adapt the prepared essay to

the needs of the actual question, and the stereotyped irrelevant answers therefore were assessed accordingly. (Chief Examiner's Report, Southern Universities Joint Board, summer 1982)

The SCP, then, offered teachers both an alternative course content and a different approach to teaching history. An assessment pattern was devised which attempted to minimize the traditional emphasis on memorizing and regurgitation, emphasizing instead the acquisition of historical concepts and skills. I want now to look at the nature of teachers' responses to, and implementation of, this Schools Council course.

A CASE STUDY

The data reported here are from a much larger study of the influence of examinations on secondary school teaching (Hammersley and Scarth, 1986). This study used qualitative and quantitative techniques to compare the teaching on different courses (those assessed only by examinations; those assessed by examination and coursework; those assessed by course work only; and pre-examination courses). Eleven humanities teachers in five schools were studied. Here I shall focus on two teachers who both worked in the same large co-educational comprehensive school. The school offered two history courses: SCP O-level to a selected group of top-ability pupils; and Oxford Board British and Economic History (O-level and CSE) to all other pupils.

The comparison between these teachers is intended to illustrate two kinds of response to curriculum innovation which involves strong assessment elements. The data do not, nor are they intended to, fully characterise all possible reactions to change in the teaching profession. However, the forms of response reported here may well have resonance not only for the area of history but for other subject areas too, where large national schemes have been launched (e.g. Geography for the Young School Leavers; Nuffield Science; Schools Council Integrated Science Project). Finally, the case studies also carry messages for GCSE which, in its form of implementation, shares common ground with the centre-periphery model of curriculum innovation used by SCP.

Teacher 1 had been at the school since 1981, when he was appointed as second-in-charge in the department. The following year he was made head of department. Data were collected in one of his SCP groups from when the course started in the pupils' fourth year to midway through their fifth year.

In general, the teacher liked the Schools Council emphasis on skills as part of an evidence-based approach to history. However, he had grave misgivings about the quantity of material to be covered on the course. In an interview after his first half term of teaching SCP, he commented upon the amount of factual material in the course:

> The problem is that there is such a lot of information to actually learn before you can actually get on to the process of interpretation.

He explained this on the basis that:

> The project team had very little, if any, actual teaching experience in comprehensive schools and they didn't really understand the practical difficulties of teaching the full age range. (Fieldnotes)

Later in the same conversation he claimed that, for pupils, the course had '50% more work relative to others'. This perception of the course, supported by comments from pupils as well as from colleagues, appears to have been fairly stable. For example, towards the end of that academic year he returned to the same theme:

> The amount of work they have to do is staggering because there is no way you can really answer questions, those detailed questions on the medicine paper or the questions on Elizabethan England unless they have done an awful lot of notes. And that is really going against what the course is meant to be about. (Interview)

Teacher 1 believed that the SCP course involved more work for both teachers and pupils than did most other O-level courses. As he put it in an interview 'this is more like a six-term course than a five-term course'. *Medicine through Time*, in particular, was cited as the module which involved the most in terms of course material. Moreover, 'selecting out' material *not* to be covered was difficult:

> At the end of the day they've got to answer some fairly difficult questions on that, now they can't answer the essay questions unless we've gone fully through those three books. (Interview)

Teacher 1 also questioned whether the evidence-based approach was genuinely 'new' to history teaching. On the importance of developing in pupils an awareness of bias and the skills needed to interpret sources, he suggested that 'good history teachers were doing this many years ago. I mean there is nothing new in that at all'. Similarly on the *History around Us* module he claimed that:

> Traditionally local history courses have inevitably tended towards the sources and any grammar school history teacher worth his salt would introduce objects and artefacts. (Interview)

Teacher 1 was, then, critical of the quantity of course content and of its presentation as a new form of history teaching.

As regards assessment, he generally liked the division of marks between examination and coursework. He had noticed that the nature of the questions on Paper 1 had changed over the years:

> The first papers, 1978 and 1977, they tended to have questions that were very very straightforward on them. Questions that were divided into separate parts with an easy part – what was the date of this or what was published on this date, what was the name of it? just factual recall – to more analytical questions. Whereas now they are trying, I think, to bring in this overall analytical and comparative sort of approach that doesn't allow perhaps so much of pure recall in response to questions. (Interview)

However, in his view, there remained a tension in Paper 1 between recall of facts and historical analysis, and he believed that the balance was still in favour of recall:

> 'At the end of the day it really is a very thinly disguised straight examination course'. (Interview)

The same point was reiterated during a staff-room conversation:

> The overall atmosphere about the unit [*Elizabethan England*] is not that different really from what we would be doing anyway in a good, reasonably taught examination course. (Fieldnotes)

This teacher also taught on the Social and Economic O-level course, which he believed was actually better suited to his form of teaching:

> I'm not entirely sure that my teaching is the sort of teaching that best relates necessarily to the Schools Council approach, I'm better suited I think to the Social and Economic-type course. (Interview)

One reason for this, he explained, was his training as a teacher:

> I think that inevitably one's teaching tends towards the sort of training and experience that one has. I was trained, if you like, in a grammar school and this is the environment in which I learnt to teach, so it's very difficult to change your style, whole style of teaching. My practice is not necessarily a *bad* practice, but it is a more traditionally oriented one I would say. (Interview)

Indeed, in the classroom, he gave much emphasis to traditional techniques. All his lessons involved notes or dictation and as the course progressed the amount of pupil participation (in the form of discussion or answering questions) decreased rapidly (Hammersley and Scarth, 1986). He continually stressed the importance of learning details and memorizing facts. For example, after the O-level 'mock' examinations in the fifth year he spent much of the follow-up lesson going over the 'facts':

> It is important to make sure you know the facts [. . .] many of you simply did not have your facts right and that just will not do [. . .] there is no substitute I'm afraid for sitting down and learning this information. (Lesson transcript)

Teacher 1's perception of the SCP course seems complex. He regarded the course as simply what good history teachers had always done. He saw the balance within the course towards recall of facts rather than interpretation of evidence and his teaching was orientated to this approach. However, he saw his own style of teaching having been trained in the grammar school ethos, as being too traditional for the SCP.

Teacher 2 had worked in the school rather longer than his colleague, and had taught the SCP course since 1977. His view of the SCP course was very different to that of Teacher 1.

When he first began teaching the course Teacher 2 had little idea of its philosophy or practical implications. He attended a number of courses to discover more about the SCP and his initial thoughts were of the extra work involved:

> I thought 'this is going to be very difficult' and it did involve me in a lot of re-thinking of the way in which I'd been teaching. (Interview)

However, once immersed in the course, he found that he liked the new approach to history teaching. In an early interview he characterized the SCP approach as being 'more analytical, so that the kids have to think'. And he believed that it could be applied to all ability ranges:

> The brighter kids, but even lower down the ability range, they're being asked to analyse, to think why this happened, what was the role of this particular individual, looking at primary and secondary sources and thinking about the two. (Interview)

Later in the school year when Teacher 2 was interviewed again he repeated this perception of the SCP philosophy:

> I would say it aims to, it attempts to teach the children how to start being historians, rather than simply to regurgitate a set of facts in sort of chronological order, which is what the traditional O-level and the traditional history teaching has always been in the past. So it attempts to teach the children the rudiments of how to approach the solving of problems in

history. Interpreting evidence, using evidence, analysing evidence. (Interview)

Like Teacher 1, he had some reservations about the quantity of material to be covered, especially on the medicine section of the course. Nevertheless, he thought that the contents of the different modules allowed for teaching which was significantly different to that on other O-level history courses:

> I've taught on the Social and Economic course and I've also taught on the 20th Century Course and I would say that the Schools Council is infinitely more demanding on the teacher [. . .] I think you can get away with not doing very much on the Social and Economic course [. . .] You cannot get away with not doing very much on the Schools Council course. (Interview)

He developed this line of thought a little later in the interview:

> I can imagine some teachers teaching a course, the Social and Economic course, incredibly monotonously, doing the same thing every lesson, lesson after lesson after lesson. I did this, that was the course I did a O-level, and it was just simply a question of me going along to the lesson, the teacher sat down, virtually dictating, or going through his notes, you writing as much as you could down in rough and then he'd say right, your homework tonight is to do this essay. And you'd go away and do the essay, hand it in, he'd mark it, give it back to you and then carry on doing the same thing. And that happened day in, day out for two years. (Interview)

This extract is worth citing at length because it illustrates in a very graphic way the manner in which this teacher perceived teaching on traditional history courses and, by contrast, the virtues of the SCP. His classroom practice was, in many respects, very different from that of Teacher 1. Though he still used notes and dictation, he did not rely solely on these to transmit information; other techniques such as filmstrips and slides were also used. Moreover, his greatest concern was that pupils grasped the importance of interpreting evidence. For example, in the follow-up lesson to the 'mock' O-level examination, he stressed the importance of analysis. In relation to a question on Elizabeth I he said:

> If you had made *that* point, the fact that one cannot get a true picture about Elizabeth just from these two extracts, I think you would stand a much better chance of getting your marks. So, as in so many cases, there is not one answer [. . .] there is not one true answer for all this, but if you analyse and justify your answer in a sure and sensible and analytical way you will get a very good mark. (Lesson transcript)

There seems little doubt that Teacher 2 was in favour of the Schools Council course. It was a course which, in his view, would shift the balance of emphasis in history teaching away from recall and memory work towards a more skill-based, analytical approach.

Teacher 1 and Teacher 2 had quite different attitudes, then, towards the SCP. Teacher 2 regarded the course as having brought benefits to history teaching; Teacher 1 was much more critical. Indeed, Teacher 1 subsequently decided, as head of department, to drop the SCP course, keeping only the more traditional British Social and Economic Mode 1 examination course.

CONCLUSION

When discussing reforms such as the GCSE it is important not to overestimate the influence examinations have on teachers. We actually know little about the extent to which examinations can, and do, shape schooling. Many claims are made (Whitty, 1978; Broadfoot, 1979, 1984) but systematic investigation is rare (Scarth, 1983, 1984; Hammersley and Scarth, 1986). One thing that the case study makes clear is that teachers' responses to a syllabus such as the SCP may be very diverse. Teachers' perceptions of a course philosophy may vary, as may their ideas about what a course requires and the teaching strategies necessary to meet these requirements. Even in the same school, as the case study illustrates, there can be big differences between teachers in attitude and teaching style. Teachers are not 'controlled' by the examination system, though examinations may influence their behaviour in particular respects.

What I am suggesting is that the language of central 'control' and teacher 'autonomy' which has been used in relation to GCSE examinations (Macintosh, 1985, Nuttall, 1985) while useful in certain aspects, may also be misleading. An increase in central control does not necessarily imply that teachers will have less autonomy. Control is not simply exercised from the centre. There are more local sources of control too, such as LEAs, headteachers, heads of departments, parents and last, but certainly not least, pupils. All these sources have some control over teachers, and their influence may be very different to that of the 'centre'. (The issue of comprehensive reorganization provides an example of how the DES, LEAs and parents may have conflicting views about what secondary schools should teach and how they should teach it.)

However control is even more complex than this. Teachers are not passive subjects of controlling forces. They may even be able to play some sources of power off against others. For example, when faced with pressures to innovate, teachers may use the pressure of examinations as a rationale for continuing with the status quo. And, more than this, teachers may be able to exercise some choice about the kind of control they will be subject to. As we saw in the case study, heads of department sometimes choose an examination course which exerts greater control over them than do alternative courses. While this may be justified in terms of examination results, the underlying motives may have more to do with the relationship between the pedagogic implications of the syllabus and the teachers' own teaching style. The point is, then, that teachers are subject to a variety of influences, and not just to control from the centre. Moreover, their responses to such influences is diverse and not simply passive.

The GCSE has undoubtedly led to some changes in schools, the administration is now very different for one thing. But whether the form of teaching we find in classrooms will be altered in any significant way is open to doubt. Regardless of Nuttall's anxiety about teachers' lack of control over assessment, ultimately it is still the teacher in the relative isolation of the classroom who makes effective decisions about the curriculum. And, as the data from the Schools Council course illustrate, how teachers implement the curriculum seems to depend as much on a variety of local factors as it does on the examination system.

ACKNOWLEDGEMENT AND EXPLANATION

I am grateful to Martyn Hammersley and Tim Horton for their comments on an earlier draft of this article.

The data reported in the case study are drawn from different sources. 'Fieldnotes' were written by the researcher as soon after an event as possible; 'transcripts' were obtained from tape-recorded interviews with the teachers; and 'lesson transcripts' were obtained from tape-recorded lessons.

REFERENCES

Ballard, M. (Ed.) (1970) *New Movements in the Study and Teaching of History*, Temple Smith, London

Bowe, R. and Whitty, G. (1983) A question of content and control: recent conflicts over the nature of school examinations at 16+. In M. Hammersley and A. Hargreaves (1983) *Curriculum Practice: Some Sociological Case Studies*, Falmer Press, London

Bossert, S. (1979) *Tasks and Social Relationships in Classrooms*, Cambridge University Press, Cambridge

Broadfoot, P. (1979) *Assessments, Schools and Society*, Methuen, London

Broadfoot, P. (1984) *Selection, Certification and Control: Social Issues in Educational Assessment*, Falmer Press, London

Brown, R. and Daniels, C. (1983) History in danger: revisited, *Times Educational Supplement*, 9 December, p. 29

Fullan, M. (1981) Research on the implementation of educational change, *Research in Sociology of Education and Socialization*, Vol. 2

Hammersley, M. and Scarth, J. (1986) The impact of examinations on secondary school teaching. Unpublished report

Joseph, Sir Keith (1984) The value of history in the curriculum. Address given to the Historical Association's conference, February 1984, reported as 'History's unique contribution', *Times Educational Supplement*, 17 February, p. 32

Macintosh, H. G. (1979) Schools Council Project History 13–16: the CSE examination, some problems of assessment, *Teaching History*, June and October, Nos. 24 and 25

Macintosh, H. G. (1985) The GCSE and the future, *Forum*, London, Vol. 28, No. 1, pp. 7–9

Nuttall, D. (1984) Doomsday or a new dawn? The prospects for a common system of examining at 16+. In P. Broadfoot (1984) *Selection, Certification and Control: Social Issues in Educational Assessment*, Falmer Press, London

Nuttall, D. (1985) Evaluating progress towards the GCSE. Paper given at the Annual Conference of the British Educational Research Association, August–September 1985

Price, M. (1968) History in danger, *History*, Vol. 53, No. 179, pp. 342–347

Rogers, P. J. (1978) *The New History*, Pamphlet No. 44, Historical Association

Scarth, J. (1983) Teachers' school-based experiences of examining. In M. Hammersley and A. Hargreaves (1983) *Curriculum Practice: Some Sociological Case Studies*, Falmer Press, London

Scarth, J. (1984) Teachers' attitudes to examining: a case study. In P. Broadfoot (1984) *Selection, Certification and Control: Social Issues in Educational Assessment*, Falmer Press, London

Shemilt, D. J. (1980) *History 13–16 Evaluation Study*, Holmes McDougall, Edinburgh

Torrance, H. (1985) Current prospects for school-based examining, *Educational Review*, Vol. 37, No. 1, pp. 39–51

Whitty, G. (1978) School examinations and the politics of school knowledge. In L. Barton and R. Meighan (1978) *Sociological Interpretations of Schooling and Classrooms*, Nafferton Books, Driffield

Chapter 14
GCSE AND SCHOOL-BASED CURRICULUM DEVELOPMENT
Harry Torrance (*University of Southampton*)

INTRODUCTION

The argument for a common school-leaving examination revolved upon the need for administrative rationalization and educational development. A common examination would save schools and local authorities from having to provide, and pay entry fees for, numerous, potentially overlapping, examination courses. It would also relieve teachers and pupils of the burden of having to take difficult strategic decisions about entering for the CSE or GCE, with all the concomitant implications for curriculum differentiation and subsequent life-chances. However, such positive arguments were voiced more cautiously as the emerging outline of the new GCSE came more firmly into focus. Nuttall (1984) suggested that the GCSE was gaining a more favourable hearing from the DES than hitherto because the new examination could be used to increase central control over the secondary curriculum. Similar arguments were put forward by Bowe and Whitty (1984), and both they and Nuttall pointed to the potential demise of Mode 3 examinations under the new national criteria as evidence of the negative impact the GCSE would have on local initiatives and particularly on school-based curriculum development. They argued that the national criteria would be so tightly defined that the scope for alternative syllabuses submitted through Mode 3 would be very limited and any changes secured would be only marginal.

A key feature of the national criteria is the inclusion of school-based assessment – the marking of coursework and practical work by teachers. Supporters of the GCSE might therefore suggest that the best element of Mode 3 – teacher involvement in assessment – has been retained. It can be argued that flexibility and the potential for curriculum development have been preserved because coursework frees teachers and pupils from the narrow pursuit of cramming for examinations. A Secondary Examinations Council pamphlet (SEC, 1985a) draws attention to the many curricular benefits of coursework assessment as well as to the variety of reasons why it might make an examination more valid and reliable. However, a centrally orchestrated extension of school-based assessment need not necessarily and of itself lead to an extension of school-based curriculum development. Teachers may find themselves in the position of unwilling conscripts, marking coursework against objectives and criteria defined and determined by others (Torrance, 1985a).

The issue falls into parts: first, the room for manoeuvre which the general and national (subject-specific) criteria allow, i.e. the extent to which alternative titles and syllabuses can be introduced; second, the sort of practices – particularly with regard to moderation – that are likely to emerge for conducting coursework assessment within mainstream group-based schemes. A detailed examination of the evidence seems to bear out Nuttall's initial foreboding, reiterated in a recent conference paper (Nuttall, 1985).

GOVERNMENT INTENTIONS

The government's general intentions were made clear in both the White Paper *Better Schools* (DES, 1985a) and the Secretaries of State's foreword to the General Criteria (DES, 1985b). The White Paper stated that the government's intention was to 'secure greater clarity about the objectives and content of the curriculum' and to 'reform the examinations system and improve assessment so that they *promote* more effectively the objectives of the curriculum' (p. 8, emphasis added). The White Paper went on to make it plain that 'National criteria are needed in order to ensure that syllabuses in given subjects have sufficient content in common' (p. 30), while 'Grade criteria [. . .] will define the main aspects of each subject which the examinations will be designed to test' (p. 31). The government established a quango – the Secondary Examinations Council (SEC) – directly appointed by the Secretary of State, 'to supervise the operation of examinations taken by pupils during the years of compulsory schooling' (p. 29) and envisaged the role of the SEC's counterpart – the School Curriculum Development Committee (SCDC) – as '*not* to advise the Government of matters of curriculum policy; it has, rather, an important role in *securing* on the ground *the changes* which will need to follow from the establishment of curricular policies' (p. 28, emphasis added). Likewise the Secretaries of State saw publication of the National Criteria as an 'historic step', representing, they claim, 'nationally agreed statements on course objectives, content, and assessment methods' (DES, 1985b, foreword). The thinking behind the introduction of the GCSE, then had two main strands. First, an objectives model of curriculum planning was employed to promote the development of consensus, or perhaps to legitimate the exclusion of dissent; second, the vocabulary of criterion-referencing was used to define curriculum content by defining standards of performance.

THE NATIONAL CRITERIA

The national criteria documents range in length from 5 pages for social science to 39 pages for science (25 of which are specimen syllabus material). The average length of the documents produced by the various working parties is 10 to 11 pages. Each follows a similar pattern with sections on aims, assessment objectives, core content and assessment weighting (the proportion of marks to be awarded to each element of the examination). Some of the sections on core content and assessment weightings are very detailed indeed (for example, science), and are presented quite prescriptively. In chemistry, for example, 'The minimum core content defined in this section will be present in all GCSE chemistry syllabuses' (national criteria for chemistry, p. 4); in biology, 'Any syllabus bearing the title biology must include the minimum core content set out below' (national criteria for biology, p. 3). In mathematics 15 aims and 17 assessment objectives are specified; this is followed by lists of core content for different courses leading to the award of different grades. Thus:

> The content of List 1 must be included in all syllabuses which bear the title Mathematics. It should constitute almost the whole of the syllabus content for any examination on the results of which the great majority of candidates is expected to be awarded grades E, F or G.
>
> The content of both List 1 and List 2 must be included in the syllabus for any examination which can lead to the award of grade C. (national criteria for mathematics, p. 3).

What we have here, then, is a statement of intent which, even without detailed grade criteria, goes well beyond any general agreement of broad objectives.

Furthermore, the principle of differentiation that underlies such specific instructions is applicable to every subject. The reason given for introducing differentiation is 'that candidates across the ability range are given opportunities to demonstrate their knowledge, abilities and achievements; that is, to show what they know, understand and can do' (DES, 1985b, p. 2). The aim is to make assessment a positive experience, with candidates rewarded for what they can do, rather than counfounded by what they cannot. This assumes, of course, that 'ability' is an unchangeable individual characteristic rather than a function of interacting variables such as motivation and interest upon which teachers (and curriculum development!) might have some positive impact. In practice, implementing the principle of differentiation is likely only to reinstitutionalize the divide between the GCE and CSE. This is especially so because 'the GCE boards will have responsibility within the Examining Groups for maintaining the standards of grades A to C; the CSE boards will have a corresponding responsibility with regards to grades D to G' (DES, 1985b, p. 1). The principle of differentiation could be adhered to by a judicious combination of differentiated questions within papers and individualized coursework assignments, thus leaving open the possibility for change and development. However, a number of key subjects – French, mathematics, biology, physics, chemistry and science – stipulate that differentiation must be achieved by different pupils sitting different papers with grade restrictions on syllabuses which do not adhere to this. For example:

> A differentiated scheme of assessment involving alternative components for candidates of different levels of ability must be used for all syllabuses on which the complete range of grades may be awarded. It is expected that schemes which allow all candidates to be assessed on totally common papers will be restricted to the limited range of grades. (national criteria for biology, p. 6; cf. also SEC, 1985b)

Examining Groups and schools alike, then are coming under direct central prescription. Of course, the Secretaries of State did not write the national criteria – they only 'approved' them – and it is reasonable to suppose that they do command considerable support, at least at certain levels in the Examining Groups, LEA advisory services, the Inspectorate and so forth. It could even be argued that the national criteria embody the best aspects of recent curriculum development, taking on board ideas from older projects such as Schools Council 13–16 History and Geography for the Young School Leaver, along with more recent developments such as APU Science and the Cockcroft Report in Mathematics.

CURRICULAR FLEXIBILITY AT EXAMINATION GROUP AND SCHOOL LEVEL

But to return to the issue of school-based curriculum development and local responsiveness, whether or not one supports the 'core content' of particular subjects, scope for local initiative seems limited. The new system involves both the implementation of a series of curricular innovations through reform of the secondary examinations system and the control of future local development. Although the national criteria are supposed to be reviewed and updated regularly, the difficulties inherent in this process are underlined by the fact that the first 20 subjects took four years to develop in the first place. Thus the use of national criteria as an instrument for curriculum development seems both cumbersome and crude, while also engendering many problems of implementation. The scope available to teachers to bring about change hinges on two key factors – the possibility of introducing new titles and (probably far more important for the majority of teachers) the procedures for moderating school-assessed elements.

EXAMINATION TITLES

One way in which local initiatives can be accommodated is through the development of alternative syllabuses and alternative examination titles. However, in general new titles will still have to accord with the national criteria (various modern languages with those of French, for example; sociology with social science, geology with science, etc.). Those that do not are likely to prove extremely marginal. Developing new courses does not get around the problem that the core curriculum – what is supposedly 'really important' – has been identified and defined in advance. In any case, all Examining Groups are under an injunction to 'avoid the unnecessary proliferation of subject titles and syllabuses', and such titles as are approved 'must be broad enough to cover the range of subject content likely to be included in different syllabuses in the same subject area' (DES, 1985b, p. 3). Examining Groups already find this difficult to comply with, as would individual schools or teachers wishing to submit Mode 3 proposals. A more fundamental problem is that all proposals have to be couched in the language of aims and objectives. Thus alternative approaches to curriculum development and alternative ways of thinking about curricular problems are proscribed (for example, the identification of worthwhile tasks which may have unpredictable outcomes, cf. Stenhouse, 1975). Similarly, because the General Criteria construe review and development in terms of subject titles, whole-school cross-curricular development is likely to be very difficult to articulate appropriately, and even more difficult to realize in practice. Integrated studies are likely to become enmeshed in bureaucratic discussions of whether they fall under one title or another and thus which national criteria they have to meet.

MODERATION OF COURSEWORK

For most teachers, however, the crucial issue – a litmus test of the flexibility of the new arrangements – is moderation. A responsive approach to moderation could provide the mechanism for teachers to gain considerable experience in curriculum development and evaluation; a narrow grade-monitoring approach is unlikely to contribute to either curricular flexibility or professional development. The evidence so far is not encouraging. The General Criteria state that moderation can be carried out by inspection or by statistical manipulation (DES, 1985b, p. 6), though little is made of the problems inherent in statistical moderation. Attention is drawn to the fact that for statistical moderation to be valid, i.e. for internal assessment to be altered by reference to a moderating instrument (usually the final paper), an 'acceptable relationship' must exist between the internal and external assessments. But this problem is then passed over as if such a relationship is easy to establish, when in fact one of the principal justifications for course-work assessment is that, unlike assessment by final papers, it tests different things in different ways. To employ statistical moderation is to risk completely devaluing the coursework element with all the consequences for teaching which that would entail.

Also, no mention is made of moderation by consensus whereby groups of teachers would come together on a regional basis to discuss each other's work. Such an arrangement could be covered by the term 'inspection' of course, and it may be that consensus moderation by local consortia of teachers will be implemented under this general heading. But without specific encouragement Examining Groups may well think that consensus moderation is too expensive and that the potential in-service benefits of teachers discussing each other's coursework products and methods should be the responsibility of the LEAs rather than themselves. At least one group – the Southern Examining Group – does envisage consensus moderation being distinguishable from inspection (i.e. from individual moderators visiting individual schools). Even so, whether the group employs consensus or inspection, it must work within further prescriptions laid down by the General Criteria. These state not only that teachers and moderators must agree on the criteria they use for marking (an obvious point) but also that such an agreement must be determined in advance and imposed from above, rather than, for example, being generated by discussion of the evidence – the coursework – produced:

> The same assessment criteria should [. . .] be used by the teacher and moderator [. . .] clear guidance must be provided to both the teacher and

the moderator as to the qualities to be taken into account and the relative weight to be attached to them. (DES, 1985b), p. 9)

So, for example, the Southern Examining Group state:

The Group will provide criteria for assessment, and the teacher or lecturer is required to mark his or her own pupils according to those criteria. (SEG, 1985, p. 5)

Teachers and moderators alike are trapped, then, into a static, monitorial relationship rather than a dynamic and developmental one.

AN ALTERNATIVE MODEL

In practice such injunctions are likely to prove unworkable. Hard-pressed teachers and moderators will do what they can to make the system work without too many disputes and appeals. Compromise and negotiation are likely to abound since, even when clear criteria are available for marking, experienced teachers and examiners often disagree over whether a particular piece of work meets the criteria or not (Jones, 1982; Torrance, 1985b). The control exercised over teachers will therefore not be absolute. Unfortunately, the benefits of a more flexible approach to moderation are not likely to accrue either. Such an approach would place as much, if not more, emphasis on the development of teachers' assessment skills and on the relationship between assessment, curriculum and teaching methods as on the growing but ultimately rather unproductive task of monitoring marks and grades. The 'effective follow-through and support' which the government itself recognized would be important for GCSE in-service training (DES, 1984), but about which it has had little to say and for which it has provided no funds, could be accomplished if it were to become an integral part of the examining and moderating process itself. If Examining Groups chose to capitalize on the experience of consensus and of inspection moderation which most CSE Boards already have (Torrance, 1982, 1985b) and if they were prepared to argue for broader discussion of objectives and marking criteria on the grounds of the validity of resultant grades and the professional development of teachers, then a more flexible model of moderation might yet emerge. Such a model would involve Examining Groups liaising with local authorities over in-service provision and specifically over the setting up and funding of local consortia of teachers and networks of visiting moderators. The key feature for moderation procedures would be maintaining regular and continuing contacts with and between schools throughout the duration of GCSE courses, rather than merely sampling and in effect re-marking coursework products as a one-off exercise at the end of a course. A continuing dialogue about curriculum and teaching methods could then follow. In-school evaluation and curriculum development would have a mechanism by which soundly based argument and negotiation would have a place in moderation. Likewise less-experienced teachers in need of continuing support rather than end-of-course inspection would be given help.

SCHOOL-BASED CURRICULUM DEVELOPMENT IN THE LONGER TERM

Finally, the question of in-service training for the GCSE also raises longer-term issues about the role of the teacher in curriculum development and the relationship between in-service training and curriculum analysis. A programme of in-service training specifically linked to the GCSE was set up in 1985 with the specific intention of introducing all heads of department to GCSE (Phase 2) and ensuring that they could then train their colleagues (Phase 3). However, this 'cascade' model of in-service training has been construed and interpreted too mechanistically – as the dissemination of information and the provision of new skills – and despite the best intentions of individuals involved in the programme, its long-term impact is unlikely to be a particularly effective one because effectiveness will depend on achieving a continuing dialogue, as outlined above. Closely circumscribed and mechanistically implemented in-service provision in the field of curriculum and assessment could lead to a narrowing of the role which teachers perceive themselves to have in curriculum development – with in-service provision seen in terms of equipping teachers to carry out technical tasks defined and designed by others, rather than encouraging them to reflect on curricular provision and how it might be improved. The point made earlier about the single-subject nature of the GCSE underlines this concern, with such scope as schools have to engage in a fundamental review of their intentions and provision being restricted to the realm of pre-vocational education through mechanisms such as the Certificate of Pre-Vocational Education (CPVE). Yet even within this newly emerging field the government is proposing to limit its development by funding training programmes directly, via the Manpower Services Commission (MSC) for teachers involved in the CPVE and in the Technical and Vocational Education Initiative (TVEI). The 1985 White Paper stated that additional specifically focused in-service provision would 'advance' the government's aims and

the Manpower Services Commission had been invited to administer a scheme for this purpose [. . .] the in-service training grants scheme [. . .] is facilitating the release of teachers to courses of training for the CPVE as well as for other pre-vocational teaching. (DES, 1985a, pp. 17, 36)

Hartley (1985), discussing similar developments in Scotland, suggested that:

the content in INSET courses will be confined to matters of pedagogical competence, thereby avoiding any wider analysis of education [. . .] this will reduce the professional teacher to a mere technician [. . .]. (p. 118)

CONCLUSION

In terms of our discussion of school-based curriculum development, then, the problem presented by current government initiatives is twofold. First, such development as might take place will be highly circumscribed by the General and National Criteria. Second, the capacity of teachers to think broadly and reflectively about educational provision in the longer term may be under threat, as in-service provision is seen more and more in terms of equipping teachers with specific skills to teach in predefined curricular areas, rather than as a way of encouraging teachers to analyse curricular problems and develop novel and responsive curricular provision.

I have suggested above and elsewhere (Torrance 1985a, 1985b) that in practice teachers and examiners will muddle through. The daily demands of teaching, marking and moderating will mediate the impact of central prescriptions. But the lost opportunity to operationalize local interpretation and adaption of broad general aims and to learn from local experience via locally based evaluation and validation schemes could prove costly. If Examining Groups developed their moderating procedures along the lines outlined above, engaging in a continuing dialogue with schools rather than a one-off monitoring exercise and paying attention to the processes of assessment and the interaction of assessment, curriculum and pedagogy, some of the many potential benefits of teacher involvement in assessment might yet be realized. It remains to be seen whether this becomes the case.

REFERENCES

Bowe, R. and Whitty, G. (1984) Teachers, boards and standards: the attack on school-based assessment in English public examinations at 16+. In P. Broadfoot (1984) *Selection, Certification and Control*, Falmer Press, London

DES (1984) In-service support for GCSE teachers. Letter from Sir Keith Joseph to Secondary Examinations Council, 21 December

DES (1985a) *Better Schools*, HMSO, London

DES (1985b) *General Certificate of Secondary Education. National Criteria* and *General Criteria*, HMSO, London

Hartley, D. (1985) Bureaucracy and professionalism: the new 'hidden curriculum' for teachers in Scotland, *Journal of Education for Teaching*, Vol. 11, No. 2 pp. 107–119

Jones, A. (1982) Educational objectives and public examinations. Paper presented to the annual meeting of the British Educational Research Association, St Andrews

Nuttall, D (1984) Doomsday or new dawn? The prospects for a common system of examining at 16+. In P. Broadfoot (1984) *Selection, Certification and Control*, Falmer Press, London

Nuttall, D. (1985) Evaluating progress towards the GCSE. Paper presented to the annual meeting of the British Educational Research Association, Sheffield

SEC (1985a) *Coursework Assessment in GCSE*, SEC, London

SEC (1985b) *Differentiated Assessment in GCSE*, SEC, London

Southern Examining Group (1985) *Moderation of Centre Assessed Components in GCSE Examinations*, SEG, Aldershot

Stenhouse, L. (1975) *An Introduction to Curriculum Research and Development*, Heinemann, London

Torrance, H. (1982) *Mode 3 Examining: Six Case Studies*, Longmans, York

Torrance, H. (1985a) Current prospects for school-based examining, *Educational Review*, Vol. 37, No. 1, pp. 39–51

Torrance, H. (1985b) *Case-Studies in School-Based Examining*, Department of Education, Southampton University

SECTION IV:

PROBLEMS AND PROSPECTS

Chapter 15
GCSE AND THE NEW VOCATIONALISM
Ian McNay (*Open University*)

INTRODUCTION

When I was an undergraduate some 20 years ago one of the things which caused me to switch from studying English literature to applied linguistics and modern use of language was being set a vacation essay asking for a comparison between Pope's *Essay on Man* and Wordsworth's *Prelude*. I believed there was no basis for comparison: they were the products of different contexts, of different cultures. I feel the same way about GCSE and vocationalism.

I want here to suggest why, to those committed to a relevant as well as a rigorous education, the GCSE is a disappointing anachronism, which doesn't fit with vocational or pre-vocational criteria exemplified through other contemporary school based developments for 14–18-year-olds such as TVEI and CPVE. I make comparison with Scotland (in favour of the Scots), and take an eschatological gaze into a crystal ball.

THE VOCATIONAL TRADITION

First, why *new* vocationalism in the chapter title? It's a voguish phrase, but there's nothing new about vocationalism. It has a long tradition. Prince Charles's comments on the risk of Britain assuming fourth-rate nation status echo those of his great-grandfather, Albert, after the Great Exhibition of 1851. The period of GCSE development has coincided with the centenary of the Samuelson Reports which urged a more vocational school curriculum to counter competition from better trained and better capitalized nations – Germany and the USA – who were overtaking the UK in economic terms. As Edwards points out:

At times of crisis, it is not uncommon to seek educational causes rather than engage in a wider analysis which might suggest financially or politically costlier solutions. (Edwards, 1983)

So nothing has changed there either!

The long-term pessimism about the depth of the economic crisis and, particularly, the extent of long-term unemployment among young people may mean that the message of the capability movement (Burgess, 1986) has found its time, though Dale claims that the aims of the new vocationalism:

> [. . .] differ somewhat from those typically found in education–employment discussions due to the shadow of extremely high levels of youth unemployment and the possibility that they might be permanent. The aims are not confined to training young people for jobs but also include the need to adjust them to a new status, somewhere between work and non-work. (Dale, 1985)

This preparation for unemployment is, then, one 'new' element in the vocational curriculum – the only one, according to Dale – and adds confusion to the previous dilemma over aims: is vocational education to enable people to get a job, or to make them able to do it? There has been another new element (though it had its harbingers), not in curriculum content, but in control: the extent of the determined intervention in detailed curriculum issues by a central government committed to Victorian values and headed by a daughter of trade. The role of MSC and the development of TVEI as the second major curriculum initiative for the pre-16 groups alongside GCSE parallels the sponsorship of the polytechnics under the LEAs 20 years ago as a vocational, socially responsive and accountable balance to the academic and autonomous universities. The Robbins Report of 1963 remains as a last and best monument to the liberal academic tradition in higher education. It remains largely unimplemented and its plea for a unitary system was specifically rejected only two years later by Crosland's articulation of the plural (misnamed 'binary') system. GCSE can be seen, similarly, as a final attempt to adjust the classical approach to cater for everybody or at least 90 per cent according to Sir Keith Joseph, before the instrumental barbarian hordes establish an alternative empire.

EQUIVOCATION

Government commitment to vocationalism has not been unequivocal. It has, for example, protected traditional sixth forms from vocational contagion through tertiary reorganization. The Green Paper which formed the basis of the 'great debate' (DES, 1977) included two aims for secondary education which disappeared after the debate was concluded. *The School Curriculum* (DES, 1981) did not include:

> To help children to appreciate how the nation earns and maintains its standard of living, and properly to esteem the essential role of industry and commerce in this process;

> To provide a basis of mathematical, scientific and technical knowledge, enabling boys and girls to learn the essential skills needed in a fast-changing world of work. (DES, 1977)

Yet Sir Keith Joseph, in his speech to the 1984 North of England Education Conference, reasserted these two aims:

> [. . .] the curriculum should be relevant to the real world and to the pupils' experience of it. Judged by that test, HMI reports show that much of what many pupils are now asked to learn is clutter. The test means, for example, that the curriculum should contain an adequate practical element and promote practical capability for all pupils, not just those who are labelled 'non-academic'; that the technical and vocational aspect of school learning should have its proper place; and that all pupils should be introduced to the economic and other foundations of our society.

How far does GCSE development, as we can see it at present, reflect this? Craft Design and Technology is included in the 'top twenty' subjects for which subject-specific criteria have been prepared, presumably absorbing Technical Drawing, which had 61 000 entries in England in 1982 compared to 14 000 for CDT. Cookery, which had 50 000, has disappeared but Latin (24 000) is retained, transmuted into Classical Studies, perhaps reflecting Sir Keith's sex as well as his background which sees causation and consequence as characteristics of the study of history, but not of science (1984 North of England speech). Business Studies and Economics are both there, though their development suggests significant overlap. But if this is the 'new' curriculum for the new vocationalism it bears a remarkably similarity to the old GCE O-level profile.

Note, then the HMI comment on certification for TVEI:

> Some projects rejected existing examinations as being too restrictive of curricular development and have found difficulty in arranging accreditation for their courses. It seems clear that, if pupils are not to be disadvantaged, certification that has national standing must be developed alongside the new courses so that it is in place when pupils need it. (DES, 1985)

If this was so with the then Mode 3 CSE flexibility, will GCSE overcome this problem?

Although the clear criteria for GCSE subjects are welcome, as is the recognition of project work and teacher-assessed course work, these gains will be mainly for the traditional academic pupil. Nowhere, yes, nowhere in *GCSE: A General Introduction*, (DES/Welsh Office, 1985a) nor in the *General Criteria* (DES/Welsh Office, 1985b) are 'employment', 'jobs' or any synonyms mentioned, nor are any vocational objectives stated.

There is a euphemistic circumlocution in *A General Introduction* which avoids mentioning employment, or perhaps more importantly unemployment, by referring to the target group as including 'those who plan to leave full-time education at age 16' (para. 7), and an almost paranthetical recognition that supplementary criteria will be needed for vocational and pre-vocational courses (para. 24), offered mainly, it is implied, by bodies other than CSE/GCE boards. This non-vocational context is emphasized in the *General Criteria*: paragraph 11 looks forward for the academically inclined in recording the intention of the exam as being 'to serve as a basis for further study and for entry to training'. For those not staying in the system, but hoping to enter the job market, the perspective is reversed and the standard setters for the system look inwards and backwards 'to record what those leaving full-time education at 16+ have achieved'. In short, introspective, retrospective, summative.

Wallace, in an examination of the early experiments within TVEI, sees GCSE and CPVE as fundamentally different and highlights the dilemmas facing schools:

> [CPVE] [. . .] comes from an entirely different horse-box from GCSE, although from the same stable [. . .] Both horses – GCSE and CPVE – have the same owner. They are running in the same race. It is not yet clear which horse the owner is backing. [. . .] We have to face [. . .] the difficulty of finding compatibility between the GCSE principle of single-subject based examinations and the CPVE principle of a whole curriculum. The choice facing schools [. . .] seems to be stark. They either use GCSE and the Low Achievers Projects as the basis for the curriculum and its validation of all their pupils, ignoring CPVE, or they divide the year group at 14, probably into three groups: GCSE for the ablest and parallel GCSE and CPVE curricula for the average and below. The only other compromise would be a combination of GCSE subjects and a part-time CPVE. This would not avoid the needs for a fundamental choice to be made by schools. It would only blur the edges. It is unfortunate that schools should have to face such a choice. (Wallace, 1985)

Wallace underlines the government's equivocation by noting that GCSE and A-levels are not included in the government's review of (vocational) qualifications at 16+ with a view to their rationalization. The CVCP (1985) have contributed to future academic drift by their statement discouraging study of vocational subjects such as computing and business studies by those hoping to enter university.

A CONFLICT OF CRITERIA

What, then, are the characteristics of the GCSE proposals which make them incompatible with the criteria for vocational and pre-vocational courses? Some have been mentioned already; in this section I wish to elaborate these and extend the list. In certain instances comparisons are made with the proposals for a new standard grade qualification in Scotland which developed following the Munn and Dunning Reports (SED, 1977a, 1977b) and was planned to be introduced at the same time as GCSE, and for a similar audience.

Its prime characteristic is that it is subject-based, and this leads to deficiencies when seen from a vocational perspective, i.e. being subject-based implies, or may require, that it does not have several of the characteristics of a vocational course. The subject/discipline basis of the academic tradition has long been under attack. In higher education, Becher, Embling and Kogan (1978) reject it because few real problems are susceptible to solutions drawn from a single discipline perspective. This suggests that the welcome innovation of an aim to develop problem-solving skills via GCSE may have the seeds of its own destruction built into the framework designed to achieve it.

In primary schools, since Plowden, and in lower secondary schools the subject structure has been broken down, ironically in some cases because of major Schools Council projects. Pring (1980) notes that in a subject based structure 'each subject will very likely to be taught separately without much reference to the others'. The subject-based structure, therefore, lacks integration, except, perhaps of material within the subject boundaries. For the post-16 group Pring thinks this is not enough:

> to meet many of the new demands upon the 16 to 19 sector one may need to think outside purely subject terms in a more integrated way. Instead of thinking of students attending different courses within different subject areas it may be more appropriate to think in terms of a single course integrating different parts.

The distinction between subject-based courses and an integrated course is not a clear one, mainly because the word 'integration' covers a wide range of possible organizational arrangements. However, the important question is: what is to be the integrating element? Is it a major subject for which other subjects provide relevant skills, understandings, information and are therefore subordinate to it? It is a theme that needs to be explored from different disciplinary angles? Is it a certain core of studies from which spring a variety of options? (Pring, 1986)

Proposals for the GCSE fail to answer any of these questions, and, therefore, move forward out of step with other curriculum initiatives within the school sector, failing to match the criteria for vocational preparation.

> The content and aims of vocational preparation are derived as much from the perceived needs of the young people themselves as from a predetermined range of disciplines; and the schemes accordingly demand an integrated approach to the planning of content. (Farley, 1983)

Response to 'the perceived needs of the young people', which implies local flexibility is discouraged by the tone, if not the wording, of basic GCSE publications from government which anticipate a substantial reduction in diversity of syllabuses, not only because of the grouping of exam boards but because 'the requirement that all syllabuses and assessment systems must comply with the national criteria is expected further to reduce the number of syllabuses' (DES/Welsh Office, 1985a). And the Examining Groups, acting in consultation with the Secondary Examinations Council, are expected to avoid the unnecessary proliferation of subject titles and of syllabuses (DES/Welsh Office, 1985b). So the principle of local decisions to enhance relevance is sacrificed to that of central control to promote rigour, and diversity and flexibility give way to 'rationalization' to promote efficiency.

Yet the SEC's partner, writing jointly with the FEU on *Supporting TVEI* is urging the opposite:

> [. . .] if, as FEU and SCDC believe, education should be student-centred and curriculum-led (rather than organisation- or resource-led) the essential is to meet students' needs in the most effective way [. . .] in devising these schemes, consideration should be given to the concept of a negotiated curriculum based on individual students' needs and wishes, taking into account their strengths and weaknesses and the ways these relate to their future aims [. . .] TVEI provides an opportunity to devise new forms of accreditation. (FEU/SCDC, 1985, pp. 4–5)

The report specifically rejects a subject-based curriculum, criticizes the attitudes of the GCE boards and barely recognizes GCSE in its section on accreditation.

Yet even within an academic, centrally controlled, subject-based, constrained-range curriculum an integrating device can easily be devised. BEC did it with cross modular assignments; SEC could do it with, for example, a 'general studies' concept which could test competence in transferring skills beyond the confines of a single subject; identify different perspectives to contribute to problem-solving approaches; incorporate topics not covered in the subject curriculum and allow competence-learning from work experience to be demonstrated. It would support the GCSE requirement that 'all syllabuses should be designed to help candidates to understand the subject's relationship to other areas of study' (DES/Welsh Office, 1985b).

This would overcome another weakness in the GCSE proposals: the discouragement of inter-disciplinarity, or even multi-disciplinarity, in spite of that last quoted criterion. The *General Criteria* devote only one paragraph to inter-disciplinary integrated or modular syllabuses which accentuates the negative by dealing with safeguards and what they should not do, rather than the potential of what they could do: 'all such syllabuses must avoid superficial treatment; the spread of subject content must not be achieved at the expense of the development of skills and understanding' (DES/Welsh Office, 1985b). The values are apparent: delving into the depths is better than development across a broad base. But what has been the most prominent criticism of English school education over the last two decades?

SCOTLAND: A CONTRAST

The Scots do it better. For the new Standard Grade courses and exams introduced after the Munn and Dunning Reports (SED, 1977a, 1977b) 'a number of new multi-disciplinary courses will be introduced to enrich pupils' learning experience' (SIO, n.d.). In addition to those echoing proposals south of the border – Business Studies, Craft and Design – these include Technological Studies (a revision of the previous Engineering Science, always more esteemed by the Scots whose pantheon of heroes includes Telfer, Watt and Macadam), Health Studies, Creative and Aesthetic Studies, and Social and Vocational Skills. Not only do these echo more closely the 'areas of experience' of the HMI ('modes' in the Munn terminology) but their content is intended to give pupils 'a better opportunity to prepare for working life' (SIO, n.d.). The Scots do not, therefore, shy away from vocationalism and these courses can provide integrative bases relevant to pupils' needs because in spite of the tradition of greater central direction there is positive encouragement of local flexibility within a national framework:

National syllabuses [. . .] leave scope for local decisions about content
and/or methods [. . .] This flexibility will give individual teachers greater
opportunity to review their approach to teaching and encourage them to
find better ways of motivating their pupils and improving their performance'. (SIO, n.d.)

This flexibility extends to structural issues:

> In addition to the full two year courses [. . .] schools will be able to offer a
> variety of school-devised courses of various lengths, or short courses
> based on national guidelines [. . .] In some cases it will be possible for
> pupils to take a group of short courses which are together regarded as
> equivalent to [. . .] and which will be assessed and given an award by the
> Scottish Examination Board in the same way as a two-year course. The
> certificate may also include information received from the school about
> other short courses which a pupil has followed. (SIO, n.d.)

Again, this positive approach, and recognition of major and minor
elements within a total curriculum contrast with the uni-dimensional unit of
GCSE. Some short courses are nationally devised and related to the study
modes. Examples include: Scottish and Celtic Studies, International and
Multi-Cultural Education, Money Management, Computer Graphics, Elec-
tronics. These are also identified with existing examined subjects into which
they can be incorporated.

The Scottish proposals have two other features which I believe make them
superior to GCSE. First, they are set in the context of other initiatives and
are concerned to relate, for example, to the current modularization of
vocational education after 16 as part of the 16+ Action Plan. Second,
although there will be, as in GCSE, seven grades of award, there will, in
addition, be three levels of presentation – Foundation, General and Credit –
which allow students a pass at the designated level.

These levels of presentation make the problem of guiding students, or,
bluntly, of separating the sheep following their academic mentors from the
less acceptable goats, much easier than is anticipated in GCSE with graded
questions; has a flexibility to allow students an award above or below their
presentation level and creates the psychologically beneficial possibility of
claiming a pass at Foundation level rather than a grade F (or 6 in Scotland).

COUNTERING THE CRITICISM

The criticisms can be summarised in labelling the GCSE proposals as
subject-based rather than integrated, and academically defined rather than

work-related. Does not the traditional autonomy of the teacher allow these deficiencies to be mitigated? It is their work within the framework which can interpret good intentions into good actions. The curriculum suggestions in the staff development packages prepared at the Open University give hopes that this will be so. In Economics and Business Studies, for example, there are case studies drawn from working life and problem-solving approaches. But this is less so in other subjects; the material was prepared by those in the vanguard of curriculum development; and the limited cascade of staff development is hardly enough to change long standing attitudes (Leech, 1986). Compare the much higher spending on TRIST to support TVEI.

Teachers must start from where they are, and many are in schools where the organizational structure is subject-based which will be reinforced by GCSE, reducing the possibility of inter-subject curriculum integration. And the academic tradition dies hard: the Association of Principals of Sixth-Form Colleges regretted that those failed by the academic exam system at 16+ could not be failed by it again at 17+. In lamenting the demise of the CEE, John Glazier, the secretary of the Association is reported as saying:

> there is a clear need for an academic course for 17 year olds who have missed out [sic] on the A, B and C grades at GCSE by *one or two grades* but want to go on with a course which is different but which has a definite academic value. Otherwise we are condemning them to the Sisyphus role of pushing the GCSE uphill time and time again' (Glazier, 1986, emphasis added)

Yet CEE ran counter to the Crowther recommendations for this group over 20 years ago (Slater, 1985). The Sisyphus metaphor might be applied to those who have tried time and again to change the dominance of the academic mode over the 14–18 curriculum. I hope that in a not too distant future resisters of positive change might be seen as Knut's courtiers. But I fear I may have to wait some time. GCSE lets the little waves come, but still resists the tide.

PROSPECTIVE

But I do not believe the newly enhanced commitment to vocationalism will fade away. We have passed a watershed; a change of government is unlikely to mean much change of direction in this aspect of education policy which is common to many countries (Cerych and Neave, 1983). Even if youth unemployment falls because of the demographic trend reducing the size of the 16+ cohort by 30 per cent this may simply increase the job-market value of well-prepared young people. Students, even the academic elite, have long been more instrumental than their teachers (Schools Council, 1970); they and the teachers newly enthused by TVEI will allow no retreat from a more relevant curriculum. Employers, too, will I believe prefer a more specifically vocational curriculum, especially one which involves a work experience – sandwich degree courses and, more recently, YTS have shown their use of such experience placements as an extended selection device.

Such students, teachers and clients will be unwilling to continue to try to fit into the procrustean assessment structure of GCSE. They are supported by HMI views in relation to TVEI which stressed the inappropriateness of CSE/GCE and the need for 'forms of accreditation [. . .] which reflect the aims of the [. . .] project' (DES, 1985). Perhaps there is a lesson here from the history of curriculum initiatives for the new sixth. The CEE was devised to provide continuity from CSE but was found wanting because it was subject based and insufficiently vocational. The FEU ideas of *A Basis for Choice* (1979) and *Vocational Preparation* (1981) were therefore incorporated in the CPVE. Just as CSE created a need for extension (upwards), so CPVE, within the framework of a 14–18 vocational and pre-vocational curriculum (if it does not drift down to 16+ as Wallace suggests), will create pressure (downwards) for preparatory feeder courses, e.g. as the universities did in promoting A-levels. The certification of the pre-vocational preparation will need to relate particularly to TVEI, but many, including those in government, believe that the quasi-totality of students pre-16 should have some vocational preparation. GCSE, in spite of claims that it should cater for 90 per cent of students, cannot provide this certification, so just as the new world of MSC and TVEI was called into existence to redress the imbalance of the old, so a new certificate will be needed to legitimate the pre-voc curriculum, nearer to the CGLI Foundation Course or BTEC initiatives which HMI found were favoured by TVEI pioneers.

There are alternative scenarios for the future. Some see 18+ becoming the *de jure* as well as the *de facto* end of compulsory education. In such a case GCSE could have the limited role outlined below; or become a pre-pre-voc qualification with real pre-voc work done after 16 though there is inescapable discontinuity because of the different approaches involved; or the UK could come into line with the rest of Europe and scrap 16+ exams altogether – a course already urged by many (Open University, 1986). In this case, and there are messages for the other two, the broad-based approaches of many lower schools could be extended upwards to continue an integrated, multi-disciplinary project-based curriculum which would be more truly pre-vocational.

The most likely development in my view is that GCSE will go the way of GCE O-levels and Scottish O-grade exams. They were devised as a terminal school-leaving qualification for those not going on to higher education – the more able were supposed to bypass them. Yet they became an intermediate selection device for those who were staying on, appropriate to an even smaller group than the 15 per cent who go into full-time higher education at 18+. They attracted a wider group because of their prestige, but GCSE may lose some of this accumulated kudos and suffer the suspicion of all new qualifications, thus allowing alternatives such as those canvassed above to gain greater parity of esteem. In such a case GCSE may drift back to being a pre-A-level screening stage offered to the 25 per cent of a cohort to whom it might be appropriate. If comprehensive schools are slowly escaping Harold Wilson's label of 'grammar schools for all', they must resist their curriculum becoming GCSE for all.

REFERENCES

Becher, T., Embling, J. and Kogan, M. (1978) *Systems of Higher Education: United Kingdom*, Interbook Inc. for the International Council for Educational Development, New York

Burgess, T. (ed.) (1986) *Education for Capability*, NFER/Nelson, Windsor

Cerych, L. and Neave, G. (1983) The vocationalization of secondary education: editorial, *European Journal of Education*, Vol. 18, No. 1, pp. 5–6

Committee of Vice-Chancellors and Principals (1985) *Choosing A-Levels for University Entrance*, CVCP, London

Dale, R. (1985) Introduction to R. Dale (1985) *Education, Training and Employment: Towards a New Vocationalism*, Pergamon, Oxford

DES (1977) *Education in Schools: A Consultative Document*, Cmnd 6869, HMSO, London

DES (1981) *The School Curriculum*, HMSO, London

DES (1985) *The Technical and Vocational Education Initiatives: Early Developments*, DES, Stanmore

DES/Welsh Office (1985a) *GCSE: A General Introduction*, HMSO, London

DES/Welsh Office (1985b) *GCSE: General Criteria*, HMSO, London

Edwards, A. (1983) The reconstruction of post-compulsory education and training in England and Wales, *European Journal of Education*, Vol. 18, No. 1, pp. 7–20

Farley, M. (1983) Trends and structural changes in English vocational education. In R. Dale (1985) *Education, Training and Employment*, Pergamon, Oxford

FEU/SCDC (1985) *Supporting TVEI*, FEU, London

Leech, A. (1986) The professionals' anxieties, *Education*, 24 January

Open University (1986) E333 *Policy-Making in Education*, Module 5 'Curriculum and Policy-Making' and associated broadcasts, Open University and BBC/OU Production Centre, Milton Keynes

Pring, R. (1980) General education and the 16–19 sector. In M. Holt (1980) *The Tertiary Sector*, Hodder & Stoughton Educational, Sevenoaks

Schools Council (1970) *Sixth-Form Pupils and Teachers*, Books for Schools, London

Scottish Education Department (1977a), *The Structure of the Curriculum in the*

Third and Fourth Years of the Scottish Secondary School, (the Munn Report), HMSO, Edinburgh

Scottish Education Department (1977b), *Assessment for All*, (the Dunning Report), HMSO, Edinburgh

Scottish Information Office (n.d.) *Scottish Secondary Education: Standard Grade*, Factsheet 29, SIO, Edinburgh

Slater, D. (1985) Sixteen to nineteen: towards a coherent policy? In M. Hughes, P. Ribbins and H. Thomas (1985) *Managing Education*, Holt, Rinehart & Wilson, London

Wallace, R. G. (1985) *Introducing Technical and Vocational Education*, Macmillan Education, Basingstoke

Chapter 16
GRADED ASSESSMENT AND THE GCSE
Roger Murphy (*University of Southampton*) and
David Pennycuick (*University of Sussex*)

GRADED ASSESSMENT AS AN ALTERNATIVE TO GCSE

An interesting aspect of the final stages of the development of the GCSE examination was the existence of parallel (or at least concurrent) alternative assessment initiatives. Best known among these alternative developments are the profiling and graded assessment movements. Each had existed in its own right for a number of years (at least since the mid-1970s) but both became much more prominent at just the time when the GCSE examination was launched.

The following chapter (by Patricia Broadfoot) outlines some of the developments that have taken place within the profiling movement and draws attention to the DES's major records of achievement initiative. In one or two cases attempts have been made to incorporate graded tests (or assessments) into records of achievement projects. Such approaches are still very much at the development stage and it is too early to say whether the somewhat different philosophies of profiling and graded assessment can be linked in this way.

The development of graded assessments pre-dates the records of achievement initiative and occurred quite independently in a number of LEAs and also through various national curriculum and assessment projects. Much of this interest in graded assessments can be traced back to the rapid development and apparent success of the GOML (Graded Objectives in Modern Languages) movement in the mid- to late-1970s.

These GOML schemes were the result of largely local initiatives by groups of secondary schoolteachers dissatisfied with traditional methods of language teaching and examining. They are now in operation in many LEAs, with over 300 000 candidates each year at different levels of the various schemes. Most of the schemes cover French and German, although several other languages are represented. They are often based on functional-notional syllabuses and stress a communicative approach to language teaching.

The interest in graded assessments has spread to other subject areas and graded assessments are now being used in mathematics (e.g. in the Kent Mathematics Project), science (e.g. in the School Science Certificate, which was developed in Avon and Wiltshire), music (examinations of the Associated Board of the Royal Schools of Music), business studies (Royal Society of Arts and Pitman schemes) and physical education (various national award schemes). Development work is already in progress in other subjects (e.g. English). In some cases individual schemes are quite small and are available only in restricted areas of the country. However, Examination Boards have shown considerable interest in the development of graded assessments and their involvement, and the results of other development work, may lead to a much more widespread use of graded assessments across a further range of subject areas. Much will depend on the type of relationship that develops between graded assessments and the GCSE. Before considering this further, we will look in more detail at the characteristics of existing graded assessment schemes so that we can compare and contrast them more fully with the pattern of GCSE syllabuses and schemes of assessment.

Although individual schemes differ, typical graded assessments have three key features:

1   There is emphasis on student success.
2   The assessments are arranged in a progressive sequence of levels.
3   The tasks to be mastered by candidates are clearly specified.

Emphasis on success implies that pupils are set tasks of an appropriate level of difficulty and are entered for tests only when they are ready for them.

Graded assessments may not be suitable for all school subjects, but where they are it is claimed that the above features give them an advantage over public examinations, including the GCSE. Harding, Page and Rowell (1980, p. 2) explain that: 'The basic principles of the Graded Objectives Scheme for Modern Language Learning [. . .] were first expressed in opposition to the plans for the new public examinations to be taken at 16+.' The extent to which the GCSE will itself manifest these features remains to be seen in some cases, as, through their emphasis on differentiation, the Secondary Examinations Council are clearly trying to transform the GCE and CSE into examinations that place greater emphasis on student success by encouraging students to show what they know, understand and can do. Grade criteria may provide a more detailed specification of what is expected from candidates. To complete the comparison it also has to be said that in some GCSE subjects the model of differentiated papers that is being proposed has some similarities with tests or assessments that are based on a progressive sequence of levels. Thus, the parallels are there potentially, but they are no more than parallels and the substantial differences that exist between the developments may turn out to be even greater. At present some of the concepts of mastery, differentiation and positive achievement that have been mentioned in relation to GCSE are no more than ideals, and doubt exists about the extent to which they can be put into practice in large-scale public examinations.

The context for conducting graded assessments has been considerably different from that for conventional public examinations. This has allowed assessment practices to be developed that cannot readily be transferred to the format of such examinations, for example informality in entry procedures and flexibility in test administration. Graded assessments have often been designed for pupils whose levels of achievement are widely different. Pupils who will ultimately reach higher levels of achievement can, under a graded assessment system, proceed faster and further through the levels than their classmates. This is less easy to achieve within the GCSE system where the constraints of formal end-of-course written examinations tend to restrict the suitability of the examination to the same top 60 per cent of pupils for whom GCE and CSE previously catered (although it was Sir Keith Joseph's intention for a greater percentage of candidates to reach those standards). Some graded assessment schemes have nevertheless been designed purely for low-achieving pupils. This development was recommended in the Cockcroft Report on mathematics which assumed that the most appropriate role for graded assessments was for them to be used to complement public examinations rather than to replace them.

LINKING GRADED ASSESSMENTS TO PUBLIC EXAMINATIONS

We have already said that many graded assessment schemes were set up as a deliberate alternative to public examinations. Many schemes have attempted to cater for the achievements of all pupils, including those who would normally have been entered for CSE and GCE examinations. In some cases such schemes have negotiated with Examination Boards to have some of the higher levels of their schemes certificated as Mode 3 CSE or GCE O-level examinations. There has been much heart-searching over whether such a step inevitably leads to a compromise of graded assessment principles, but some GOML schemes have proceeded in this way in order to ensure that fifth year pupils following GOML-based courses can have the opportunity to obtain public examination certificates. The extent to which such arrangements can continue under GCSE depends to a large extent on whether graded assessment schemes can meet the constraints of the GCSE national criteria and, eventually, the grade criteria. Little is known at present about the role of Mode 3 examinations within GCSE, but there are fears that the much more detailed lists of criteria and regulations associated with GCSE syllabuses and schemes of assessment may effectively stifle almost all alternative developments.

Mode 3 is not, however, the only way in which graded assessments and the GCSE could be linked. The advent of grade criteria and the principle of differentiation make great demands on teachers in terms of the coursework assessments required in all GCSE syllabuses. Graded assessment schemes may be seen as a useful basis for conducting coursework assessments that are both linked to stated criteria and tailored to the particular achievements of individual pupils. Parallels for this type of combination of graded assessment results with public examination results already exist. For example in music some A-level examinations require candidates to have passed grade V of the practical examinations of the ABRSM. In the Kent Mathematics Project there were Mode 3 CSE and Mode 2 O-level examinations for which KMP levels determined the coursework grades.

There is still much development work to be done in this area, as the nature of GCSE coursework assessment is still under discussion. It is also likely that the coursework assessments introduced in the early years of the GCSE will have to be radically revised if and when grade criteria are introduced in the 1990s. It can only be hoped that the valuable experience gained from the various elements of the graded assessment movement will not be ignored when GCSE schemes of coursework assessment are being discussed.

PRESERVING THE PRINCIPLES OF GRADED ASSESSMENT SCHEMES

The pioneers of graded assessment set out to develop a genuine alternative to the ideals and practices of GCE and CSE examinations. Many of them fear that their achievements will be lost if graded assessment becomes a mere adjunct to the GCSE scheme of assessment. There are several potential dangers in such a move.

Increased pupil motivation has been a principal aim for many graded assessment schemes, and the detailed arrangements for assessing pupils on these schemes have been worked out to optimize the chance of achieving that aim. Thus the setting of short-term attainable goals has been seen as more important than the traditional Examination Board preoccupations of standardization, comparability and reliability.

This same philosophy can be found in a number of educational reports, including the 1984 Hargreaves Report, where the proposed assessment system for sequenced short course units was planned to motivate pupils turned off by the long-term and often inappropriate goals presented by public examinations. Harrison (1982, p. 25) in his review of the early graded assessment schemes claimed that 'the momentum gained by GOML schemes is largely a result of new motivation for pupils'. Mary Warnock (1985, p. 27) has provided further strong support for this radically different approach to organizing assessment in secondary schools: 'with readily attainable targets [pupils'] motivation for the work would be vastly improved. Most would want to move on to the next grade, in their own interests'.

Whether or not schemes such as these will necessarily lead to a widespread increase in pupil motivation remains to be seen. The evidence so far is fairly inconclusive, although there have been suggestions that short-term motivational gains may diminish over time and that problems may arise where pupils fail to meet short-term goals.

Graded assessment schemes are also seen as a catalyst, a lever and/or a vehicle for curricular and pedagogical reform. In modern languages, for example, GOML schemes are a means of introducing a communicative approach to language teaching. In mathematics, KMP and SMILE are primarily task-based individualized learning programmes. In these cases, the principles of graded assessment are present and may be essential, but nevertheless are often regarded as secondary reasons for the development and operation of the schemes. Each scheme provides a learning structure which defines and stabilizes the classroom situation for both teachers and pupils, and thus assists implementation of the key reform in question. The potential for 'backwash' effects on the curriculum is a feature common to graded assessment and GCSE. In the case of the GCSE, the national criteria form the instrument by which the Secondary Examinations Council may exercise curricular influence and/or control; if grade criteria are implemented, such control will increase even further. Questions to be addressed for both graded assessment and GCSE are the degree, desirability and flexibility of these influences in each particular case.

A further principle of graded assessment schemes is mastery. This idea derives from the learning programmes developed by Bloom, Keller and others in the United States, although there are some significant differences; for example, learning units in graded assessment schemes last much longer (up to one year) than in Bloom's strategy, which proposes units lasting about two weeks.

Public examinations, on the other hand, are not based on mastery and one difficulty in relating graded assessment schemes to GCE and CSE examinations has been a method of arriving at grade boundaries which 'relies on both norm-based and criteria-based considerations' (Orr and Nuttall, 1983, p. 13). The fact that these examinations offered a wide range of grades rather than the simple success/failure borderline preferred by most, although not all, graded assessment schemes may be seen as a major factor contributing to incompatibility between the two systems. However, Harrison plays down this point:

At first sight this distinction between a series of grades on a certificate and a series of certificates for successive grades might seem to be one of the crucial differences between the once only, 'big bang' examination at the end of the course and the shorter-term assessments taken by the pupil when she is ready to pass. But the differences in the way the results are arrived at are not at all clear-cut. (Harrison, 1982, p. 29)

Nevertheless, one of the main points which graded assessment schemes have had to accept in negotiating Mode 3 proposals is in the awarding of a range of grades in the public examinations, with consequent concessions on mastery and on clarity of reporting. The advent of grade criteria in GCSE may however bring the new system more into line with graded assessment on both these points. Furthermore, as we have already noted, the GCSE examination with grade criteria and differentiated papers may be quite like a graded assessment system in many ways. One major remaining difference is likely to be that GCSE will still essentially depend upon a final examination at a fixed time, whereas in graded assessment the emphasis is on progression through a series of levels over a period of time, probably several years.

Grade criteria will hold the key to introducing into GCSE another of the principles of graded assessment, that of providing meaningful and positive descriptions of what pupils know, understand and do. In the past public examination grades have been recognized as conveying very little specific information about these things. They have provided global, largely norm-referenced, gradings of pupils. A change towards more meaningful public examination results was one of the expressed intentions of the previous Secretary of State:

We should move towards a greater degree of criterion-referencing in these examinations and away from norm-referencing. The existing system tells us a great deal about relative standards between different candidates. It tells us much less about absolute standards. We lack clear definitions of the level of knowledge and performance expected from candidates for the award of particular grades. . . . We need a reasonable assurance that pupils obtaining a particular grade will know certain things and possess certain skills or have achieved a certain competence. (Sir Keith Joseph, 1984)

However, the work completed on the draft grade criteria is only a fairly modest first step towards a possible radical revision of GCSE schemes of assessment and grade awarding procedures, and there can be little hope of further progress without a further major research and development exercise. Again, such an exercise would do well to take on board the experience developed through the graded assessment schemes (Murphy, 1986).

GRADED ASSESSMENT APPROACHES TO MAKING RESULTS MORE MEANINGFUL

Most, although not all, graded assessment schemes award certificates at each level, and in many cases these include descriptions of varying degrees of specificity of what successful candidates can do. These descriptions might consist of a list of topic areas covered, or a list of objectives expressed in behavioural terms. Often what appears on certificates is amplified in syllabus documents. Analysis of syllabus content in terms of behavioural objectives has been carried to considerable lengths in some of the current large-scale commissioned developments.

The question of how meaningful graded assessment certificate descriptions are gives rise to several issues. One is the degree of precision which is required. Another is the extent to which the acquired skills are context-free. Nuttall and Goldstein refer to this issue and give the example of a child who can calculate a percentage being presumed to be able to do so in all practical contexts.

What many researchers have realised is that such symbolically defined skills do not necessarily transfer from one situation to another, since performance depends upon disposition and motivation, for example, as well as 'competence', and indeed that the autonomous existence of a 'skill' is itself rather a slippery notion. (Nuttall and Goldstein, 1984, p. 7)

One has only to glance at the backs of some certificates to see that this is a problem for graded assessment. Can pupils who can 'buy food and drink in a café' (GOALS, Graded Objectives for Achievement in Language Skills, French Level 1) order what they want, or only those items for which the vocabulary has been learnt? Can they do it in France, or only in the simulated café of the GOALS test? If other pupils can 'measure lengths under a metre to the nearest mm' (School Science Certificate, Level 1) can they do this when required in a craft lesson or at home, or only in the science laboratory in order to get their certificate? Can they measure a tiger's head with a tape-measure? More seriously, for how long will they *retain* their skills?

The problem is not specific to graded assessments but applies wherever a description of 'what the candidate can do' is required – say, on a record of achievement or in a GCSE examination. Pennycuick and Murphy (1986) discuss the construct validity of certificate descriptions and argue that there is a tension between simultaneous requirements to be precise and concise. The same skill listed in two schemes may in practice mean two quite different things.

> The difficulty with such out-of-context descriptions is that they are too poorly defined to ensure comparability, and the more precisely defined they become the more rooted in a context they become. (Nuttall and Goldstein, 1984, p. 6)

A complicating factor is that, within a single scheme, a pupil may not have actually acquired a particular skill listed on his or her certificate, since in many cases there is mark aggregation, and pass marks, although higher than in many traditional examinations, are still far from 100 per cent.

There are several possible approaches to the problems posed by the testing and description of context-free skills. One possibility is to pursue criterion-referencing as proposed by Popham (1978). The necessary behavioural-objective definitions and test-item conditions could not be presented on certificates but could be available elsewhere for those requiring fuller information. A second approach would be to relax, or even abandon, the urge to define and assess skills independent of context and to revert to topic-based syllabus definitions. Descriptions of candidate attainment would then be of the form 'x has covered the following syllabus and has scored y per cent on the test'. The recently introduced AEB Basic Skills Tests appear to fall into this category. As a third possibility, Massey and Newbould, writing about records of achievement, make the ingenious suggestion that:

> A weak definition of the generalisability of skills can perhaps be employed which may be of 'real life' application. We may attest in the record of achievement to a student's ability to demonstrate a skill having been exposed to appropriate familiarisation with a context. The user is hereby implicitly invited to assume that the skill could be demonstrated in

different contexts given whatever (re-) familiarisation was necessary. (Massey and Newbould, 1986)

Fourthly, we could simply admit the difficulties by including a suitable set of caveats on each certificate and adopting the position that, although there are these problems, the attempts which have been made to describe a pupil's skills/abilities/competence/attainment/performance/standard, although imperfect, represent considerable progress on the lack of information provided by GCE or CSE results. A fifth possibility is for teachers to assess skills, defined by explicit criteria, on several occasions over a period of time. Criteria could then be assessed in different contexts. This possibility is being explored by several groups (e.g. OCEA) which are developing criterion-referenced assessments in various subject areas.

CONCLUSIONS

In the preceding sections we have reviewed areas of conflict and agreement between the ideals and current state of graded assessments and the GCSE. In the light of these contrasts there seem to be many common ideals although in many ways some graded assessment schemes are much closer to meeting those ideals than the GCSE schemes of assessment that have been developed so far.

The GCSE has got much more to learn from the graded assessment movement than has so far been recognized. The problem is that the GCSE has been based on the experience and practices of those who were centrally involved in GCE and CSE. Graded assessments grew out of a disillusionment with those examinations and their assessment procedures. Adopting such a radical change of emphasis may be beyond the scope of the present fairly modest reorganization of the public examination system. We have indicated a number of potential dangers in including graded assessment schemes under the umbrella of the GCSE. However at a time when there are so many alternative assessment initiatives, graded assessments will decline unless they are linked to at least one of them. Some LEAs are already considering graded assessment results as part of a school-leaving record of achievement for all pupils by 1990. In these cases much depends on the conclusions that the DES will draw from the records of achievement pilot projects in different LEAs.

The graded assessment movement has been a very significant, substantially teacher-led development within secondary schools in Britain since 1970. Much experience has been developed that is highly relevant to the aims of the GCSE examination and the records of achievement initiative. The next period will reveal whether or not graded assessments can survive to play an even more significant role within or alongside whatever emerges from these alternative curriculum and assessment initiatives.

REFERENCES

Harding, A., Page, B., and Rowell, S. (1980) *Graded Objectives in Modern Languages*, Centre for Information on Language Teaching and Research, London

Harrison, A. (1982) *Review of Graded Tests*, Schools Council Examinations Bulletin 41, Methuen Educational, London

Massey, A. and Newbould, C. (1986) Qualitative records of achievement for school leavers, *Cambridge Journal of Education*, in press

Murphy, R. (1986) The emperor has no clothes: grade criteria and the GCSE. In C. Gipps (ed.) *The GCSE: An Uncommon Exam*, Bedford Way Papers (in press), London

Nuttall, D. L. and Goldstein, H. (1984) Profiles and graded tests: the technical issues. In *Profiles in Action*, FEU, London

Orr, L. and Nuttall, D. L. (1983) *Determining Standards in the Proposed Single System of Examining at 16+*, Comparability in Examinations Occasional Paper 2, Schools Council

Pennycuick, D. B. and Murphy, R. J. L. (1986) Mastery, validity and comparability issues in relation to graded assessment schemes, *Studies in Educational Evaluation*, in press

Popham, W. J. (1978) *Criterion-Referenced Measurement*, Prentice-Hall, Eaglewood Cliffs, NJ

Warnock, M. (1985) A secondary revolution, *Illustrated London News*, September

Chapter 17
RECORDS OF ACHIEVEMENT AND THE GCSE
Patricia Broadfoot (*University of Bristol*)

THE COMPONENTS OF CHANGE

This book is about the GCSE. It is about the latest update in the examination tradition that stretches back through O-level and CSE and lower School Certificate to the late 19th century. Whilst the GCSE contains many novel features, it is still an examination cast in the traditional mould – a two-year course culminating in a formal, one-off, summative testing procedure which is reported in terms of a series of grades. Whilst it is now apparent that some characteristics of the new exam such as the national subject criteria, grade criteria and a substantial component of teacher assessment are novel, none of these innovations are in themselves sufficiently radical to challenge the acceptability of this new form of examination in professional and public circles. GCSE is still, in essence, a chip off the old block.

But, in the twenty years or so during which time the movement for bringing about a common system of examining at 16+ has been gaining momentum another, very different initiative concerned with 16+ certification has also been growing. This is the initiative variously called profiling, and, more recently, records of achievement. Profiles first became a buzz-word in educational circles in the mid-1970s when, following the raising of the school-leaving age in 1972, it became increasingly apparent to both the providers and the consumers of education that it was necessary to find an alternative goal for those young people now destined to spend a considerable period in secondary schooling and for whom existing certification procedures were not suitable. In a sense this constituted a re-run of the move to institute CSE some ten years before, itself a response to the pressure for certification procedures to be provided for those large numbers of young people excluded from potential O-level entry.

Following a number of early initiatives such as the pupil profiles project in Scotland (SCRE, 1977) and the Swindon Record of Personal Achievement

(Stansbury, 1980), teachers began to take up with enthusiasm the idea of pupil profiles, and studies conducted in the early 1980s (e.g. Balogh, 1982; Goacher, 1983) testify to the rapid spread of profiling schemes in individual institutions. In 1984 the National Profiling Network was established by Dorset Local Education Authority and the Southern Region Examinations Board in order to provide for information exchange between those involved in profiling in their individual institutions and authorities. Currently the network has over 200 individual schemes registered with it. This is testimony to the continuing enthusism and support for profiling among individual institutions and teachers (Pearson, 1986).

The strength of the enthusiasm for profiles, and of the arguments on which that movement is based, is reflected in the fact that in 1983 the government decided to take a policy initiative in this respect with a view to providing all young people with a record of achievement on leaving school by the end of the decade. The publication of their draft policy statement in November 1983 produced an unprecedented degree of enthusiastic support from all sections of the educational and industrial community. This encouraged the DES and the Welsh Office to produce jointly in July 1984 their policy statement on *Records of Achievement* in which they sum up the arguments for profiling as set out below:

Purposes of records of achievement. The Secretaries of State believe that there are four main purposes which records of achievement and the associated recording systems should serve. These purposes overlap to some extent.

Recognition of achievement. Records and recording systems should recognise, acknowledge and give credit for what pupils have achieved and experienced, not just in terms of results in public examinations but in other ways as well. They should do justice to pupils' own efforts and to the efforts of teachers, parents, ratepayers and taxpayers to give them a good education.

Motivation and personal development. They should contribute to pupils' personal development and progress by improving their motivation, providing encouragement and increasing their awareness of strengths, weaknesses and opportunities.

Curriculum and organisation. The recording process should help schools to identify the all round potential of their pupils and to consider how well their curriculum, teaching and organisation enable pupils to develop the general, practical and social skills which are to be recorded.

A document of record. Young people leaving school or college should take with them a short, summary document of record which is recognised and valued by employers and institutions of further and higher education. This should provide a more rounded picture of candidates for jobs or courses than can be provided by a list of examination results, thus helping potential users to decide how candidates could best be employed, or for which jobs, training schemes or courses they are likely to be suitable. (DES/Welsh Office, 1984)

The DES has now instituted a programme of nine pilot schemes in some twenty-two authorities in England and Wales, on the basis of which it hopes to draw up national guidelines for records of achievement before the end of the decade. Records of achievement thus rank alongside GCSE as one of the major assessment initiatives of this decade, and the two initiatives are likely to find themselves increasingly running in parallel in individual institutions. This article is about the significance of such a concatenation of development activity, and of the potential for links between them. In the first part of the chapter I shall look at some of the similarities which characterize both policies and then turn to somé of the contradictions which may well result in significant problems for both of the initiatives.

This analysis will also require us to take into consideration still other developments in assessment procedures which are currently taking place. In particular it is necessary to consider the graded assessment movement, variously called graded tests or graduated assessments, and experiments with modular accreditation techniques. Whilst graded assessment procedures differ in many respects from one scheme to another, they generally have the characteristics set out in the extract below, namely an approach to curriculum and assessment which involves the periodic assessment of mastery of a particular level of skill, building up into some four or five levels of performance in any one subject where the top level is often linked to a particular grade in the GCSE. Graded assessments have been introduced in a number of subjects, notably Maths, Science and Modern Languages, in many different local authorities during the 1980s (see Murphy and Penny-cuick, Chapter 16 in this book). Their development was considerably spurred by the publication of the Cockcroft Report, *Mathematics Counts*, in 1982, which argued the importance of relatively short-term achievable objectives related to specific criteria if motivation was to be maintained among lower achieving pupils. Research has shown that whilst there are considerable difficulties in implementing such an approach to curriculum and assessment within the existing school organization, many such initiatives have indeed produced considerably improved levels of motivation among pupils, and in particular the numbers opting for Modern Languages has significantly increased as a result of such schemes (Pennycuick, 1985).

Modular accreditation builds on a number of the same principles in seeking to break down an extended – normally two-year – curricular programme into a series of much shorter curriculum units or modules, often of some 40 hours each. Like graded assessments, these curricular units have built into them specific learning objectives and explicitly defined criteria of what will constitute mastery of those objectives. Normally pupils work through particular modules and then are awarded either a pass or fail only.

It is beyond the scope of this paper to consider in detail the strengths and weaknesses of this whole constellation of assessment initiatives. Rather, the thrust of this chapter will be to consider not the initiatives themselves, but the interrelationship between them. The need to evaluate the impact of particular innovations is now well recognized. Indeed the DES has currently funded a major research project designed to evaluate the pilot schemes it has funded, for example for developing records of achievement. What is much less likely to be recognized is the importance of considering the *interrelationship between these various initiatives*, and certainly there is no sign as yet that such an evaluation is to take place. What this neglect may mean is the substance of this chapter.

A GROWING CONSENSUS

GCSE, records of achievement, graded assessments and modular accreditation schemes are all manifestations of a growing consensus that quite new principles need to be enshrined in certification procedures. The traditional examination emphasized recall of knowledge, external assessment, the ranking of pupils one against another and, perhaps most important of all, the provision of information suitable for selection. However the changes that have taken place in society in recent decades, which have resulted in the rapid growth of youth unemployment, have resulted in a greatly reduced importance of certification at 16+ for selection purposes. A small minority of young people now leave school at 16 to go directly into employment. Most will stay on for an extra year at school or go into some form of further training. The choice of that training is often more a question of guidance than of selection. Because of this, wide support has developed for assessment procedures which are more positive and educational in their orientation. In particular, there is a concern to design certification procedures that:

1   allow a much wider range of achievements to be acknowledged;
2   make it possible for all pupils to have some testimony to their achievement;
3   will give information to potential customers which is relevant to both theirs and the pupils' needs;

4   enhance pupils' motivation and self-esteem by providing them with an achievable goal;
5   facilitate large-scale curriculum change by being both formative and summative in its impact.

In place of a 'sudden death', once-and-for-all examination, is growing support for assessment which is an integral part of day-to-day teaching and learning, which helps pupils come to understand themselves better, as well as helping the outside world, subsequently, to understand the qualities of that pupil. These arguments are summed up in the list below, taken from Murphy and Pennycuick:

Desirable characteristics of new certification procedures:
1   Wider range of achievements.
2   Meaningful and positive descriptions of *all* pupils' achievements.
3   Promote curriculum development.
4   Enhance teacher morale and pupil motivation.
5   Harmonious relationship between assessment, curriculum and teaching in individual schools. (Murphy and Pennycuick, 1985)

Both the GCSE and records of achievement enshrine many of these principles. They are designed to be positive in their orientation, emphasizing what pupils 'know, understand and can do'. For this reason both are oriented towards criterion-referenced assessment in which achievement is measured against a given level of performance, rather than simply against the performance of other pupils. In many cases, the grade criteria of the GCSE are very similar in format to the comments and grid statements used on many profiles. Both approaches, too, emphasize the importance of teacher assessment. Teacher assessment constitutes a significant part of the assessment in all but one of the 20 principal GCSE subjects. Records of achievement clearly depend fundamentally on teacher-based assessment. Both procedures reflect current government policy concerns with increasing vocationalism and preparation for working life at the pre-16 stage. Thus there is a marked emphasis on the assessment of skills rather than knowledge in both initiatives. For this reason, both the GCSE and records of achievement are likely to require a much wider range of assessment techniques to be employed than was normal for more knowledge-based examinations, with oral and practical components figuring significantly. Finally, both initiatives are capable of incorporating graded assessment information; in the case of the GCSE this is most likely to be in the form of an equation on the graded assessment certificate; in the case of records of achievement such attainment will simply be recorded on the record. Nevertheless, both provide the opportunity for such attainments to be formally recognized.

GROWING CONTRADICTIONS

These similarities emphasize the coherence of the contemporary assessment climate. However, if we look a little more closely, we can also detect major contradictions between the two initiatives under discussion. First of all, whilst records of achievement aim to describe individuals in a sufficiently detailed way to prevent comparison between them, GCSE results are still basically hierarchical in that a series of grades is involved and pupils will still be comparable according to the grade achieved. GCSE, like its predecessors, remains predominantly a 'sudden death' examination, for which there are little or no formative components, whereas the provision of regular feedback and review is becoming increasingly fundamental to profiling schemes. GCSE is also still largely concerned with subject learning and excludes assessment of any personal or work-related qualities and skills, which is a determining characteristic of records of achievement. In addition, whilst many, if not all, children are likely to take GCSE examinations in the most popular subjects of Maths and English, the examination is primarily designed for the same population as covered by O-level and CSE, namely the top 60 or so per cent. There will still be a significant number of young people who can hope for little success from it, in stark contrast to the commitment that *all* pupils should receive a record of achievement. Lastly, the GCSE requires pupils to wait for the length of a two-year course before they can know whether they have been successful, whereas a record of achievement is only the most recent and perhaps summarizing statement of progress which the pupils themselves have monitored and recorded.

These contradictions between GCSE and records of achievement may be explained quite simply since they reflect a fundamental tension in the purpose of school assessment itself. It is widely recognized among those involved with education that one of the most significant aspects of certification procedures is that aspects of educational endeavour which are not assessed are unlikely to be taken seriously by either teachers or pupils. During the course of the last hundred years or so educationists have progressively sold out to those who have imposed upon the education system the responsibility for attesting attainment and selecting suitable candidates. In the later stages of schooling in particular, examination-oriented work in all aspects of the curriculum – aesthetic, physical, intellectual, personal, social, moral and spiritual – and the urgent necessity to cover the syllabus has resulted in many teachers feeling constrained in their choice of teaching method and objectives. As a result, it is common to find many of the widely supported objectives not explicitly recognized in assessment procedures. In consequence, these objectives have been relegated, in many cases, to the hidden curriculum and pastoral concerns.

This argument is well made by the recent report on the curriculum and organization of ILEA secondary schools, which distinguishes between four aspects of achievement (ILEA, 1984). The first – written expression, knowledge retention, organization of material and so on – is that normally measured in conventional examinations. The second relates more to skills – the application of that knowledge, practical, oral and investigative, which figures in some examinations to a greater or lesser extent. The third element covers personal and social skills, communication and relationships, the ability to work in groups and personal qualities such as initiative, responsibility, self-reliance and leadership. The fourth concerns the capacity to understand and cope with one's own experiences in terms of, for example, motivation and commitment, perseverance, self-confidence and the constructive acceptance of failure. Neither of these dimensions are explicitly recognized in public examinations. Yet few educationists would argue that they do not figure in their overall goals for what they wish pupils to achieve or that they do not impinge fundamentally on pupils' potential success or failure. The point at issue is whether such affective, and essentially subjective, aspects of educational and personal development can or should be subjected to formal recognition in the certification process. Those responsible for designing and piloting GCSE have taken the view that such aspects are not appropriate, whereas the records-of-achievement lobby would argue that they are among the most important aspects of progress to record, because in the end they are likely to be the most fundamental.

In short, the contradiction between GCSE and records of achievement hinges on the question of whether the priority for 16+ assessment should be the provision of reliable information which has high predictability for the purposes of selection, or whether the primary purpose should be to reflect what has been achieved in relation to the whole range of educational goals that a school may set for itself. This is essentially a distinction between assessment as an integral part of the curriculum and assessment which is designed primarily to be a form of communication serving the needs of the outside world.

The question therefore arises as to what the implications of this contradiction might be. The answer to this question needs to be couched as much in curriculum terms as in assessment terms. That is to say, whether or not records of achievement can coexist alongside GCSE or will, in the end, be defeated by it or perhaps even itself defeat GCSE will depend very largely on the curricular developments of the next few years. Alongside the current assessment revolution are equally radical curriculum initiatives associated with a whole alphabet soup of acronyms. The Technical and Vocational Education Initiative (TVEI) and the Certificate of Pre-Vocational Education (CPVE) are good examples of this. Both of these curriculum initiatives are associated with trying to increase the component of industrially and vocationally relevant education taking place in schools. Where TVEI is designed to be only a part of a pupil's curriculum in the 14–18 age range, the CPVE has, in contrast, been designed explicitly for that section of the pupil population for whom A-levels are inappropriate, but who wish to achieve some further, more vocationally relevant qualification at school.

Despite their differences, however, both initiatives are associated with an increasing interest in modular-based curriculum provision, and with forms of assessment which can take into account the wide range of outcomes they are designed to achieve. There is considerable variety among different TVEI schemes up and down the country but most, if not all, involve some element of profiling. In the CPVE this element of profiling is explicitly required in the arrangements for the course. The effect of innovations such as TVEI and CPVE is likely to be more far-reaching than is at present possible to envisage. If, as seems likely, the trend continues for the curricular domination of individual subjects to be supplemented or indeed replaced by a more fluid organization of learning in terms of either modular units or work-related competencies, this is also likely to strengthen the support for records of achievement with or without a component of external examination.

Having said this, the question still remains as to whether such records, particularly where associated with unfamiliar curricular approaches, can successfully challenge the status of external examination certificates in the eyes of the world at large, especially parents and employers. Any answer to this question must necessarily be qualified in terms of the type of profile concerned. It is relatively easy, for example, to envisage a complementary relationship between a profiling system which is primarily confined to the pastoral work of a school which will then complement the more conventional assessment procedures. This might be in the form of a joint certificate such as that envisaged in the Oxford Certificate of Educational Achievement (Willmott, 1986), or in the form of a supplementary record such as that provided by 'pupils' personal recording', for example (De Groot, 1986).

It is also possible to envisage successful record of achievement schemes where these are confined to a particular course such as the CPVE or some of the other externally accredited vocational courses. These are essentially isolated from the main curricular work of a school and for those involved in them the profile has its own validity in the same way that, for example, RSA typing examinations have always done. However, the government initiative of 1984, in which it commits itself to a policy of records of achievement for all pupils, states:

> The Secretaries of State believe that the internal processes of reporting, recording and discussion between teacher and pupil should cover a pupil's progress and activities across the whole educational programme of the school, both in the classroom and outside, and possibly activities outside the school as well. Regular dialogue between teacher and pupil will be important for the fulfilment of the first three purposes of records discussed earlier.
>
> The summary document of record which young people take with them when leaving school or college will need to include two main components:
>
> (i) Information, other than academic successes, which throws light on personal achievements and characteristics;
>
> (ii) Evidence of attainment in academic subjects and practical skills, including any graded results in public examinations.
>
> The summary document will need to be short, clear and concise if employers and others are to make use of it. It cannot reproduce all the recording and reporting which has taken place during a pupil's years of secondary education. It should however be based on this internal recording and reporting, and this relationship between the internal recording and the final summary document should help to enhance the motivation and other benefits which pupils derive from the recording system. (DES, 1984)

This is likely to mean that this element of coexistence hitherto possible will become increasingly problematic. A brief review of the history of the profiling and records of achievement movement will serve to underline this point.

GOING PUBLIC: COEXISTENCE OR CONFLICT

At the outset I suggested that there has been considerable grass-roots enthusiasm to initiate profiling schemes. In the late 1970s the early pioneering initiatives such as the Scottish Pupil Profile and the Evesham Personal Achievement Record were subject to considerable diversification by the entry into the field of various further education bodies. The Further Education Unit of the DES itself published a seminal curriculum document in 1979 entitled *A Basis for Choice*, and from this radical approach to curriculum provision for further education a considerable commitment to profiling has emerged. The ideas pioneered in many of the courses which followed on from the ABC document are now central to much of the thinking behind records of achievement. These include the idea of joint review of progress by students and teachers, and the idea of centre rather than pupil accreditation as the basis for the external moderation of records of achievement.

The diversification that followed the entry of further education bodies into the field of profiling was also associated with the move for a more formal institutionalization of records of achievement. In place of the school-based, or perhaps consortia-organized, profiles of the 1970s and early 1980s, there was an increasing tendency for profiling schemes to become more formally institutionalized in either a local authority context and/or in relation to an Examination Board for the purposes of validation. Thus, in the last year or two, many Examination Boards have become involved with collections of local authorities to form profiling consortia, for example, the Northern Partnership for Records of Achievement, based on the five Examining Boards which constitute the Northern Examining Association and 22 northern LEAs, or the OCEA initiative already referred to. Significant also, in the last year or two, has been a variety of moves to evaluate the impact of records of achievement. Not only has the DES funded a major evaluation programme of its own schemes, many of the local and regional initiatives are also instituting evaluation studies.

All these data will help to inform the stage of development into which the records-of-achievement movement is now moving, namely that of nationalization following the proposals laid out in the 1984 policy statement. It is the escalation of the profiling movement from a diverse and essentially idiosyncratic set of initiatives into a development that looks likely to be rationalized in terms of National Criteria in a very similar way to that imposed on the GCSE itself which makes most problematic the relationship between the two initiatives. If we were simply talking about a supplementary form of school report, with or without external validation, it might be possible to envisage GCSE results as simply one component of such a report. If, however, as seems more likely, the current trend within the profiling movement to give increasing emphasis to the formative dimension of the process continues, then the contradiction will become increasingly pertinent.

Whereas profiles were initially envisaged as a form of school-leaving report or record, and designed to fill a gap in the existing certification procedures, it is now true to say that many, if not the majority, of those involved in such developments place their highest priority on the changes such procedures will bring about within the educational process itself. Many of the schemes currently being developed in various parts of the country are using the establishment of a record-of-achievement procedure to engage teachers in a fundamental review of their curricular goals, their teaching methods and hence their assessment criteria, with a view to stimulating a wide-ranging review of school arrangements. The kind of novel learning environment that is characteristic of the pilot CPVE schemes now being implemented, which breaks down the traditional barriers of subjects, compartmentalized lessons and didactic teaching, may well spread rapidly into other areas of the school's work. Teachers are likely to find themselves increasingly required to engage in one-to-one dialogue with individual pupils as the basis for periodic reviewing of academic and personal progress. Graded assessment and modular accreditation schemes are likely to hasten this process since they too involve the erosion of traditional subject-based teaching and curriculum boundaries and require a much greater degree of organizational flexibility and ongoing review and guidance to be provided through course tutoring if they are to be successful.

Teachers are thus likely to be faced increasingly with divergent pressures. On the one hand, GCSE requires them to develop new ways of teaching the traditional two-year subject course and, in so doing, preparing pupils with the skills required for an external exam. At the same time, they will find themselves caught up in moves to develop new organizational procedures, new teaching situations and new assessment techniques, many of which, such as one-to-one dialogue and negotiation with pupils, they will have had little or no experience of.

The problems this situation is likely to create are considerable. First, and perhaps most fundamental, is the problem of finding sufficient time. This is widely recognized as one of the biggest stumbling blocks to the successful implementation of any innovation, and particularly one such as profiling which requires teachers to find time for a new kind of activity, namely one-to-one discussion with pupils, as well as completing detailed records. In the same way, all examinations make considerable demands on teachers' time in terms of involvement in Examination Board work, running examinations in school and subsequently marking them; but an examination like GCSE, with radically new features, is likely to involve considerably more time over the next few years for teachers to become able and proficient in its procedures. Thus, time taken for GCSE will erode that available for records of achievement and vice versa.

The time problem is also related to the need for in-service training. Teachers readily admit at the present time that in most cases they have had little or no training in assessment procedures, and therefore feel they lack both the skills and the confidence to take on a more responsible role in certification. Not only will the advent of records of achievement and GCSE together make considerable demands in this respect in terms of time, it will also require teachers to engage in in-service activities for a very wide range of different assessment procedures. The potential for confusion therein is therefore considerable.

By the same token, most record-of-achievement schemes now are actively searching for some form of external accreditation through the validation of school procedures and pupils' overall programmes. The model on which GCSE is based is the more traditional one of moderation of individual pupil scripts. Thus, once again, there is considerable potential for teachers to become confused between the relative demands of these two quite different approaches to moderation and caught up in a great deal of additional work. As a consequence, they are likely to be faced with the necessity of balancing priorities – within the various demands being made upon them by the inchoate changes which characterize the present assessment climate.

In this balancing act, a number of factors are likely to be influential. One of these is pupils' attitudes to the various rival innovations, if they cannot be coordinated together. For any institution, it is likely that pupils' attitudes will constitute a significant factor in the success or otherwise of the innovation. As far as records of achievement are concerned, the attitude of pupils is likely to be even more problematic, since pupils' natural concern with the currency of their certificates, and their now well-documented tendency to see schooling largely in terms of its capacity to provide qualifications (see, for example, Turner, 1984), suggests that records of achievement may not have as immediate and enthusiastic support among pupils as they do amongst many teachers. The problem is one of the continuing dominance of traditional models of assessment at the same time as trying to introduce other models based on quite different educational premises.

CONCLUSION

The simultaneous introduction of both GCSE and records of achievement is therefore likely to render both innovations more problematic than would otherwise be the case. Goodwill, training, time, skill and pupil support are all likely to be in shorter supply than would be the case if there were not such a plethora of assessment innovations taking place at the same time. Even more fundamental than these pragmatic constraints, however, is the educational philosophy underlying the two initiatives. Whilst two innovations embodying quite different educational values attempt to coexist it is unlikely that both will be successful. Either schools will have to lend the bulk of their support to the organization and teaching forms which are associated with more traditional forms of assessment, or they will have to recognize the full implications of new forms of recording achievement and adjust their procedures accordingly.

In this chapter I have made no attempt to discuss why it should be that the DES has found itself in the situation of promulgating these various initiatives, or indeed how it sees the relationship between them. The principal explanation is likely to be that so characteristic of English educational provision, where the strength of local initiatives is also a weakness; where central government's desire to support and disseminate a variety of innovative practices at the local level can lead to confusion and contradiction in national policy-making. More cynical commentators have suggested that the government's desire to maintain traditional examinations and to introduce records of achievements as well is a re-enactment of the 'sheep and goats' mentality of the earlier tripartite system, with academic exams being preserved for the scholastic elite, and records of achievement serving the needs of the rest (Ranson, 1984). Some would go further and argue that the wide-ranging emphasis of records of achievement on recording a great variety of skills and personal qualities, as well as specific attainments, is a re-enactment of the old elementary school concern with civic virtue and Godliness as well as basic competence in the 'three R's' (Hargreaves, 1986). It is beyond the scope of this paper to address any of these arguments. It is likely that there is a germ of truth in them all. Rather, what this chapter has been concerned to make clear is that the potential impact of records of achievement, as well as that of the GCSE, cannot be determined without making reference to both initiatives.

It is certainly possible that the confluence of various tides of change in assessment policy will prove instrumental in creating a wave of sufficient magnitude to bring about a revolution in attitudes to 16+ certification; of generating a degree of momentum that no single initiative could achieve by itself. In the wake of such a wave would come the commitment to criterion-referenced, positive statements; to teacher-assessment and to a skills-oriented curriculum, identified earlier as the elements in a new certification consensus; to the principles of curriculum depth, breadth, balance and differentiation integral to the design of GCSE and also central to much of the thinking about records of achievement.

Sadly, it seems more likely that the appeal of the existing examination tradition will remain prove vastly superior to that of a novel and relatively untried procedure. If this does indeed prove to be the case, one of the most significant outcomes of the GCSE is likely to be the limitations it imposes on the parallel development of records of achievement. Experience with an earlier version of comprehensive 16+ examination north of the border where the cutting edge of educational policy has already elevated modular accreditation into a major component of post-16 certification (SED, 1984) suggests that the GCSE, like the Scottish Standard Grade, may already be obsolete, and that the hybrid offspring of the conjoining of the norm and criterion referencing pedigrees that the search for subject and grade criteria represents will satisfy no one (Munro, 1985). Many informed commentators in England also take this view that the GCSE relates to an approach to secondary school curriculum and selection which social change is rapidly rendering inappropriate (see, for example, Nuttall, 1985). If it does indeed prove to be the case that the GCSE becomes outmoded almost before it has begun, for the reasons discussed in this chapter, this will represent a tragic waste of scarce educational resources. It may also prove to be the case that failure to recognize this obsolescence sufficiently early also prevented the development potential of records of achievement being recognized. To avoid this second and ultimately much more fundamental tragedy, *the relationship between* GCSE, records of achievement and other assessment initiatives needs to become as much a matter for urgent discussion and evaluation as the initiatives themselves.

REFERENCES

Balogh, J.,(1982) *Profiles*, Schools Council, York

De Groot, R. (1986) Pupils personal records. In P. Broadfoot (1986) *Profiles and Records of Achievement: A Review of Issues and Practice*, Holt Saunders, Eastbourne

DES/Welsh Office (1984) *Records of Achievement: A Statement of Policy*, HMSO, London

FEU (1979) *A Basis for Choice*, DES, London

Goacher, B. (1983) *Recording Achievement at 16+*, Schools Council, York

Hargreaves, A. (1986) Record breakers. In P. Broadfoot (1986) *Profiles and Records of Achievement: A Review of Issues and Practice*, Holt Saunders, Eastbourne

ILEA (1984) *Improving Secondary Schools*, ILEA, London

Munro, N. (1985) The quiet reform of standard grade, *Times Educational Supplement*, 29 November, p. 5

Nuttall, D. (1985) Evaluating progress towards the GCSE. Paper given to the annual conference of the British Educational Research Association, Sheffield

Pearson, G. (1986) A network of profiles. In P. Broadfoot (1986) *Profiles and Records of Achievement: A Review of Issues and Practice*, Holt Saunders, Eastbourne

Ranson, S. (1984) Towards a tertiary tripartism: new codes of social control and the 17+. In P. Broadfoot (1984) *Selection, Certification and Control*, Falmer Press, London

SCRE (1977) *Pupils and Profiles*, Hodder & Stoughton, Edinburgh

SED (1983) *16s–18s in Scotland: A Statement of Policy*, HMSO, Edinburgh

Stansbury, D. (1980) The record of personal experience. In T. Burgess and E. Adams *Outcomes of Education*, Macmillan, London

Turner, G. (1984) Pupils' attitudes to examinations. In P. Broadfoot (1984), *Selection, Certification and Control*, Falmer Press, London

Willmott, A. (1986) The Oxford Certificate of Educational Achievement. In P. Broadfoot (1986) *Profiles and Records of Achievement: A Review of Issues and Practice*, Holt Saunders, Eastbourne

Chapter 18
THE 16+ CRITERIA

The new guidelines for the GCSE are the 'professionals' criteria', according to Sir Wilfred Cockcroft, chairman of the Secondary Examinations Council.

They represent more than two years' discussion between exam boards, teachers and Secretaries of State. Many reflect innovatory curriculum work like the Schools Council history and geography 14–18 projects. Others draw heavily on the recommendations of subject associations.

All the criteria will be reviewed regularly and the SEC sees the feat of achieving national agreement on syllabuses as proof of the criteria's flexibility. Grade-related criteria will define what each candidate will have to do to be awarded a particular grade. The grades run from A to G, with the GCE boards having special responsibility for grades A to C, while the CSE boards maintain the standards of grades D to G.

The examining groups also have a duty to redesign syllabuses which do not follow the National Criteria.

GENERAL CRITERIA

All subjects must comply with the General Criteria, including those not covered by the existing subject-specific National Criteria. The omission of a subject from the specific National Criteria below does not mean that it is less important or that examining groups cannot put forward proposals for exams in that subject.

The National Criteria are the first national exam regulations to say that syllabuses must be free of political, ethnic, sexist and other forms of bias.

Examining groups must also bear in mind the linguistic and cultural diversity of society and should try to incorporate material which reflects this. They should also consider making special provision for candidates whose mother tongue is not English.

The source for this chapter was the *Times Educational Supplement*, 29 March 1985 and 5 April 1985. Reprinted with permission.

All syllabuses must also try to help candidates relate subjects to other areas of study and to their own lives. Awareness of economic, social and political factors should be encouraged.

Differentiation is another new element. By providing papers and questions at differing levels of ability, it aims to allow candidates to show what they can do.

MATHEMATICS

Practical and investigational skills are emphasized in the criteria. Candidates should be able to apply maths to everyday problems and to science and technology. Tests should assess pupils' understanding of mathematical processes and their ability to use them to solve problems.

There is also a new stress on oral and investigational work. By 1991, all examining groups will have to offer a coursework element which will test pupils' ability to discuss mathematical ideas, and carry out mental calculations and practical work. This will have to account for at least 20 per cent of the assessment. Between 1988 and 1991, all groups will offer an optional course work scheme.

The graded lists of contents may seem fairly traditional to some teachers, but school-based assessment should allow them more scope. The original lists have also been pruned to leave the examining groups free to decide what the additional areas should be for candidates aiming at Grades A or B.

The criteria follow the Cockcroft Report's recommendation that exams must be matched to pupils' attainments and must not undermine their confidence. The criteria define three different levels of assessment based on different lists of content.

In theory, every candidate should be able to score 70 per cent, no matter which paper he or she takes. There is a considerable overlap between the differentiated papers so that late decisions can be made on exam entries.

Although using an electronic calculator is one of the assessment objectives, there is no mention of micro-computers, a surprising omission.

FRENCH

The criteria vastly increase the weighting generally given to oral assessment, listening and speaking are two of the four assessment objectives. And the stress is on communicative competence rather than, necessarily, grammatical accuracy. One of the aims is developing the ability to use French effectively for practical communication.

The other aims include:

● offering insights into the culture and civilization of French-speaking countries;

● encouraging positive attitudes to foreign language learning and to speakers of foreign languages; and

● promoting more general learning skills such as analysis, memorizing and drawing inferences.

Listening tests require authentic spoken material like announcements, weather forecasts and interviews. Reading tests should use public notices and signs, menus, brochures and, for more able pupils, magazines and newspapers likely to be read by 16-year olds.

Candidates aiming at Grade D or above should be able to write simple letters or notes, while pupils hoping to gain A or B should be able to write on a range of topics in response to a written or visual stimulus.

As for speaking, candidates aiming for lower grades should be able to answer unprepared questions on a limited range of topics, while more able pupils should be able to hold a sustained conversation on one or more subjects. There is no longer any requirement for the traditional précis, summary or prose translation.

SCIENCE

The science criteria apply to all the experimental sciences, including integrated, coordinated, combined and general science, as well as chemistry, physics and biology and applied sciences like geology and rural science.

There is a shift from the acquisition of knowledge to its application and evaluation, and practical work also has a more important role. Only 45 per cent of the total marks have been allocated to knowledge and understanding of scientific facts, terminology, apparatus and quantities.

At least 20 per cent of marks must go to the assessment of practical and experimental skills, and at least half of these must be awarded on the basis of laboratory work. Students are required to plan, conduct and interpret experiments, and to devise them to check the validity of data or generalizations.

Course work is recognized as the best way to assess practical skills; formal practical tests will only be acceptable for external candidates.

At least 15 per cent of the total marks are to be allocated to the technological applications of science and to its social, economic and environmental implications, which should 'pervade all parts of the examination'. But it will not be permissable to set questions which can be answered without appropriate scientific knowledge.

Biology

The criteria specify a minimum core of content which should account for two-thirds of the total marks. The core themes are:
- the diversity of organisms – ranging from micro-organisms to mammals;
- relationships between organisms and with the environment, such as energy flow with ecosystems and human interactions with the environment;
- the organization and maintenance of the individual – including basic cell structures and life processes in plants and animals; and
- the development of organisms and the continuity of life, including reproduction and inheritance.

The minimum core can become a full complement of content by treating specific topics at more depth and by adding other relevant topics to the core themes.

Chemistry

Experimental work and the applications of chemistry have a central role. Candidates must be able to explain the everyday uses and practical applications of chemistry and select tests, procedures and practical techniques to 'investigate the validity of interpretations, conclusions, generalizations and predictions'.

The minimum core of content includes knowledge of specific compounds and of patterns and theories, understanding chemical applications in industry and the social, economic, environmental and technological implications of chemistry, as well as carrying out experimental skills. But all of the core areas must be interrelated so that pupils can understand, for instance, the applications of chemical compounds and theories.

Physics

Experimental work and social, economic and technological applications of physics must pervade the whole syllabus.

Experimental work requires a combination of skills including: analysis, interpretation, synthesis and evaluation, and laboratory skills, including observations, manipulative skills and specific techniques.

Core content is specified in five main areas:
- matter, including the structure of an atom and states of matter;
- energy, including forms of energy, energy transfer and waves;
- interactions, including forces in equilibrium and electrical and electro-magnetic interactions;

● physical quantities, such as base and derived quantities and their units; and

● applications of physics, which must be included in the other core areas.

ENGLISH

Oral work is compulsory in the new criteria. To achieve a pass in English, candidates must pass the oral part of the exam, which has five pass grades. Oral assessment should include structured discussion, interviews and individual conversations, as well as reading aloud and delivering a talk.

Reading must include the reading of whole works of literature rather than extracts and a wide variety of literary and other material must be covered. Comprehension tests must not be confined to multiple choice tests, which are not allowed to account for more than 20 per cent of the total marks.

Course work must account for at least 20 per cent of the marks. This will allow pupils to revise their work and will encourage good writing habits, as well as giving them a chance to sample a wider variety of writing.

The assessment objectives say that candidates must show a sense of audience and an awareness of style 'in formal and informal situations'. They must also show control of paragraphing, sentence structure, punctuation and spelling.

Considering the implications of English in a multicultural society is one of the aims of the criteria.

The grade descriptions provided are rather unclear. To win a Grade F for written language, a candidate must be able to understand 'basic facts, ideas and opinions, presenting them with a degree of coherence'. A Grade C candidate will be able to order and present facts, ideas and opinion 'with a degree of clarity and accuracy'.

English Literature

English Literature shares the same aims as English and course work is also compulsory; it must make up at least 20 per cent of the total marks. Some syllabuses may be based entirely on course work.

Unseen material as well as set texts should be used to test recognition and appreciation of language and style. And there will be less emphasis on memorizing; lengthy extracts or plain texts should be permitted in the exam room.

The majority of set texts for English Literature must originally have been written in English, including American and Commonwealth writing, but works in translation are also allowed.

Candidates may also be offered a wide personal choice from the work of specific authors, themes, periods or genres.

The syllabus must include detailed study of at least two literary genres, as well as wider reading in three. Between 60 and 75 per cent of the total marks must be allocated to the detailed study of individual texts. Response to literature and appreciation of style should also be tested by unseen material.

HISTORY

The criteria demand more emphasis on historical reasoning and analysis rather than regurgitating facts. One of the aims is to promote an understanding of the nature of cause and consequence, continuity and change, similarity and difference.

Pupils will be encouraged to assess the past and to use source material to interpret events. Another aim is to develop the ability to locate and extract information from primary and secondary sources, and to detect bias and to analyse and construct a logical argument from this information.

As part of assessment, candidates will have to interpret and evaluate historical evidence which will not necessarily be related to their particular syllabus.

To achieve Grade F, candidates will have to show the obvious limitations of a piece of evidence and list some of the evidence needed to reconstruct a given historical event. For Grade C, candidates must be able to demonstrate the limitations of a piece of evidence by, for instance, pointing to generalizations or the use of emotive language.

Course work counts for at least 20 per cent of the marks. There will be a common set of papers with some differentiated elements.

There is no minimum core of content so that examining groups can devise schemes which reflect local interests. But each examining group must offer at least one syllabus which 'helps pupils towards an understanding of the intellectual, cultural, technological and political growth of the United Kingdom and of the effects of these developments on the lives of its citizens'.

CLASSICAL SUBJECTS

Different criteria apply to linguistic and non-linguistic exam courses. Syllabuses like Latin and Roman civilization will combine both types of criteria.

But in Latin and Greek courses, pupils must have studied enough literature to respond to Roman and Greek authors, as well as enough language to understand an unprepared prose passage. And they must read at least two kinds of literature from prose, poetry and drama.

Knowledge and understanding of the literature, life, history and customs of the Greek or Roman people must account for between 10 and 25 per cent of the marks in the linguistic exam.

It is up to examining groups to decide how much lexical help candidates should receive and to balance this with the difficulty of the linguistic tests. Translation must not be the only test of linguistic skills.

Coursework will count for between 20 and 50 per cent of the marks in non-linguistic subjects. It can be used to test candidates' informed, personal response to classical literature in translation.

Pupils should also show an understanding and evaluation of classical achievements, as well as an awareness of the source material from which information is derived.

Civilization should be studied through art and archaeology, as well as through other evidence. And pupils should compare their own civilization with classical civilizations and become aware of classical influences.

Knowledge and understanding should make up between 40 and 60 per cent of the marks. Evaluation, application and response should be weighted between 40 and 60 per cent, too.

GEOGRAPHY

All syllabuses must now contain physical and human elements. There is an emphasis on the relevance of geography to social issues like pollution and the marked contrast in the level of economic and technological development between and within nations.

The aims include encouraging an understanding of different cultures within our own society and elsewhere and an awareness of people's interaction with environments.

There is a strong emphasis on practical skills, which should include analysis, interpretation and use of data like maps and photographs, as well as the production of graphs and diagrams.

Fieldwork is now compulsory and must be assessed by teachers. School-based assessment should count for at least 20 per cent of the total marks.

Syllabuses must contain:

● First-hand study of a small area, preferably the student's home area;

● Study of contrasting themes within the British Isles, including population, agriculture, industry and communications;

● Consideration of the UK's relationships with wider groups of nations such as the EEC;

● Study of the geographical aspects of important social and environmental issues; and

● The interrelationship and interaction between people and their environments.

Recall, the understanding and application of skills and the use of practical skills all have the same weighting for assessment, between 20 and 40 per cent of the total marks.

SOCIAL SCIENCE

The criteria concentrate on method, process and skills rather than memory recall. Interpretation, evaluation and application of material should make up between 20 and 40 per cent of the total marks, analysis, 20 to 40 per cent, organization, 20 to 30 per cent and recall, between 20 and 35 per cent.

One of the four key content areas is the handling of data. The others are knowledge, understanding and skills in three areas: social institutions and processes, politics and government and economic awareness.

Assessment objectives stress the use of source material. They include the ability to:

● Recall, organize, analyse, interpret and evaluate social scientific knowledge; and

● Distinguish between evidence and opinion, and to recognize deficiencies such as bias and inconsistency in material.

All syllabuses must give 'due attention' to cross-cultural study as a method, and to promote awareness of cultural differences between and within societies. They must also include the implications of gender for the society and the individual.

Course work must contribute between 20 and 40 per cent to the final marks.

ECONOMICS

The criteria emphasize conceptual understanding and are not as descriptive as traditional syllabuses. Candidates must be able to explain and apply appropriate terminology, concepts and elementary theory and to distinguish between evidence and opinion.

Data response questions, testing the techniques which economists need to interpret data, must account for at least 20 per cent of the total marks. Candidates must show that they can select, analyse, interpret and apply data.

While knowledge and understanding should make up at least 40 per cent of the total marks, application of knowledge, analysis and judgement count for at least 60 per cent.

A minimum of 20 per cent of marks must also be awarded on the basis of course work, which has not generally been required before.

The core content includes:

● The functions of organizations and institutions like trade unions and banks;

● Economic activity as a means of achieving certain ends over time – for example, economic growth as a means of maximizing welfare; entrepreneurship as a means of providing income, employment, profits; public sector programmes;

● Economic variables and elementary theory – for example, supply and demand, competition and monopoly; and

● The interdependence of the parts of the British economy and its whole and the global interdependence of national economies.

CDT

There are three main titles for certification:

CDT: Design and Realization

CDT: Technology

CDT: Design and Communication.

But exam boards are free to submit proposals for other 'endorsement titles' which describe particular areas under study. Traditional skill-based subjects like metalwork and woodword which do not satisfy the criteria will have to be submitted under the general criteria and will not be entitled to the prefix 'CDT'.

The three titles have common aims, assessment objectives, grade descriptions and techniques of assessment, but separate content, and its relationship to assessment objectives is spelled out for each of the three titles. Between 30 and 50 per cent of the marks should be allocated to course work, half of which must be for practical work.

The aims include:

● Fostering awareness, understanding and expertise in those areas of creative thinking which can be expressed and developed through investigation and research, planning, designing, making and evaluating and working with materials and tools.

The assessment objectives include:

● Gathering, ordering and assessing the information relevant to the solution of practical or technological problems; and

● Analysing and producing design specifications which have been self-identified or posed by others.

HOME ECONOMICS

The criteria demand an integrated, problem-solving approach to home economics. The main assessment objective is to analyse situations by 'identifying the human needs and material factors involved, to recognize the inter-relationships of these needs and factors,' and to apply knowledge to them.

Other assessment objectives include justifying judgements and choices in the light of evidence and evaluating the effectiveness of a course of action. It will no longer be enough to make a garment; a candidate will have to show why a particular material or design was chosen.

Candidates may choose to concentrate on one or more of the major aspects of home economics – family, food, home and textiles – which will count for 60 per cent of the course. But all students must also study a common core which will be present in the main study and extend from it to the other major areas.

If the main study is the home and the theme is efficiency in household routines, then the student will have to consider the sequences for preparing food, baby-care routines and the sequencing of tasks in constructing a garment.

The common core or themes are supposed to bring the four main aspects of home economics into interaction with each other. They are: human development, health, safety and protection, efficiency, values, aesthetics and interaction with the environment.

All main studies should also include the following skills: investigation, measurement, communication, management, psycho-motor and technology.

Assessment of the core should be 'diffused' through the examination as a whole rather than assessed in separate papers. Between 30 and 50 per cent of marks should be allocated to the assessment of practical work.

RELIGIOUS STUDIES

The criteria require a broad-based study of religion which emphasizes the variety of religious faith, its place in life and the part it plays in forming human behaviour. All courses should promote an enquiring, sympathetic and critical response to the study.

All candidates should be able to show understanding of:
● Language, terms and concepts used in religion;
● The role and importance in religion of special people, writing and traditions;

● The principal beliefs of the religions studied;
● Religious and non-religious responses to contemporary moral issues;
● Questions about the meaning of life and the variety of faith; and
● Issues of belief and practice arising from the study of religion.

Candidates may either study one or two major world religions through a variety of different approaches, or make a thematic study of three major world religions under headings like 'Founders' or 'Leaders' or 'Worship' and 'Ritual'.

School-based assessment should account for between 20 and 30 per cent of the marks.

ART AND DESIGN

Art advisers have welcomed the criteria. They say that most of the aims and objectives already form the basis of current good practice in schools, but the criteria will give pupils the chance to express themselves in a far broader way. The aims include the development of manipulative skills as well as the encouragement of intuitive and analytical abilities.

There is also relief that for the first time all exams are to be scrutinized, which will ensure comparability of standards between different boards.

Some teachers may be disappointed that critical and historical studies are not an exam requirement, although one of the subject's aims is to increase understanding of the work of artists, designers, architects and craftsmen.

Other aims include the:
● Development of visual and intellectual awareness through practical skills, relevant theory and 'conscious decisions based on intuitive, analytical and synthesizing processes';
● Use of a wide range of materials and techniques in which to work and experiment; and
● Encouragement of the ability to identify and solve problems in a tactile form and relate abstract ideas to practical outcomes.

Pupils may choose to concentrate on one area from the following assessment: drawing and painting; graphics; textiles; three dimensional studies; or photography. Or they may submit work based on several areas.

Coursework should count for at least 25 per cent of the final mark.

A 'controlled test' where candidates work to a brief within a time limit, will make up at least another 25 per cent of the marks. Some schemes will allow teachers to set and assess coursework and controlled tests.

COMPUTER STUDIES

The criteria aims include:
- Fostering an awareness of what characterizes information, information processing and computer systems;
- Developing reasoning, judgement and persistence in applying, creatively, information processing technology to problems which are relevant and worthwhile to the student; and
- Developing an awareness of the ethical, social, economic and political consequences of the use of computers.

The five assessment objectives include:
- Showing a knowledge and understanding of the techniques used to solve problems;
- Using computers sensibly to produce solutions to appropriate problems and document their solutions; and
- Demonstrating a knowledge and understanding of the functions of the main hardware and software components of a computer system and their relationships with the presentation of stored data and programs.

Weightings are given to each of the assessment objectives. Differentiated papers or questions will be used in schemes of assessment.

Sixty per cent of assessment will be based on timed written papers. A candidate's use of computers can only be tested through school-based continuous assessment by teachers. Additional assessment objectives can be added to the syllabus.

The criteria are basically the same as those proposed by the GCE and CSE Boards' Joint Council in 1983.

BUSINESS STUDIES

The business studies criteria take a more detailed look at the world of work than some courses in the past. One of the aims is to 'promote knowledge and appreciations of the working world' and to encourage students to participate in society 'through group activity within the classroom and direct experience outside it'.

There must also be 'significant coverage of the roles and relationships in which the student is likely to be involved as a participant in business behaviour'.

The criteria offer an integrated course, rejecting the commerce, economics and accounting options which were first proposed. There are five essential areas of study: the external environment of the business, business structure and organization, business behaviour, people in business and aiding and controlling business activity.

Syllabuses can either be entirely based on the core content, or examining groups can offer an option based on one of the core areas which would account for 20 per cent of the syllabus.

One of the aims is to develop numeracy, literacy and discovery skills; recall of knowledge only accounts for 40 per cent of the total marks. Yet many advisers still feel that the aims are based too much on content and not enough on skills, and that the approach is too academic.

Coursework should make up between 20 and 40 per cent of the marks and might include project work or cross-modular assignments which offer students the opportunity to work together in groups.

MUSIC

The criteria are more concerned with making music and listening to it than with facts about the people who wrote it. They reject the traditional academic approach and substitute three main content areas: listening, performing and composing.

Candidates must be able to respond critically to a wide variety of styles as part of the listening test. They should be able to follow a score and identify different styles of music.

Performing unseen and unrehearsed music is another assessment objective. Candidates may sing or use any instrument they choose, and may play any style of music, including pop, folk or Afro-Caribbean.

They must also be able to sing or play as part of an ensemble as it is felt that this will give them a chance to develop their leisure interests, as well as to learn the cooperative skills needed to make music. Students must be able to improvise.

GLOSSARY OF TERMS

Aims should consist of statements setting out the educational purposes of following a course in a particular subject at GCSE.

Assessment objectives describe the skills and abilities which are measured and recorded through assessment in a particular exam subject.

Common core (syllabus): the body of subject content and the range of skills and activities which all pupils are expected to have covered.

Coursework is assessed internally by teachers for examinations. It measures and encourages the development of skills which are not easily tested in timed, written exams.

Differentiated exams/components: different parts of the exam are set at varying levels of ability to meet the needs of candidates of different levels of ability.

Grade descriptions attempt to describe the expected attainment of candidates awarded grade C and grade F in the GCSE exam. They will eventually be superseded by the grade-related criteria, which will offer more exact descriptions of what candidates must be able to do to achieve a particular grade.

INDEX